80 Years with KMB

1933-2013

Ko Tim-keung

Contents

Buses arriving at Tsui Ping Road in Kwun Tong in about 1975. Two routes (11B and 11C) departed from Tsui Ping Road to Kowloon City Ferry Bus Terminus and Wang Tau Hom respectively, passing through industrial districts such as Kwun Tong, San Po Kong and To Kwa Wan.

Foreword

Hong Kong is internationally renowned for its extensive transport network. The Kowloon Motor Bus Co. (1933) Ltd. (KMB), established 80 years ago, is the oldest transport company in Kowloon and the New Territories, operating the largest number of routes as well as covering the most extensive area.

80 years ago, the population of Hong Kong was less than 1 million with the number of people living in Kowloon and the New Territories barely making up half that number. Back then, the population of the Kowloon Peninsula was concentrated in a few districts, such as Yau Ma Tei, Kowloon City and Sham Shui Po. Sha Tin, Tai Po, Yuen Long, etc., in the New Territories were mostly farmland. The area that stretched from Kwun Tong to Diamond Hill in East Kowloon was not yet developed and there were a limited number of bus routes. The expansion of KMB came on the heels of the development of new towns and the construction of roads, providing the public with an easily accessible and convenient mode of transport. It began with satellite towns such as Tuen Mun, Yuen Long and Tsuen Wan, and later spread to new towns like Sha Tin, Tai Po and Fanling. In recent years, the expansion has reached new districts such as Ma On Shan, Tseung Kwan O and even Tung Chung (on Lantau Island). Nowadays, KMB operates around 390 bus routes, with an average of 2.6 million commuters each day.

It is evident KMB has grown with Hong Kong throughout the years, enduring some ups and downs with the city – the Japanese occupation of Hong Kong, the sudden surge in population after the war, social upheavals and natural disasters. Through all these challenges, Hong Kong has survived and prospered, and so has KMB. The company has flourished against all the odds and demonstrated that it can stand the test of time.

KMB has not only witnessed the history of Hong Kong, but has also contributed a considerable amount to the city. Mr Ko Tim-keung, this book's author, chronicles the rise of KMB, its bus route expansion and business plans from an appropriate entry point - the growth of Kowloon and the New Territories. An experienced historian, Mr

Ko has researched different aspects of Hong Kong's history and has written a number of bestsellers. He is particularly skilled in using archive data and has employed a large number of official documents to explore the relationship between the government's transport policies and the development of KMB. This work debunks certain myths about the industry and also sheds new light on bus services that many people know little about.

One interesting point made by Mr Ko is that the Hong Kong Government decided to offer franchised bus services in 1933, despite the fact that several bus companies had already been operating in Kowloon prior to that. The book explains why the tram has not been introduced in Kowloon and why double-deck buses were used only after the war. It also covers the different kinds of buses used over the years. The history of KMB is vividly delivered through Mr Ko's informative text, complemented with his personal collection of historical photos. Bus enthusiasts will be delighted by the publication of this book.

As for general readers, the book guides them through the development of KMB together with the growth of Kowloon and the New Territories. On its 80th anniversary, I sincerely wish that KMB will continue to prosper and be of great service to the residents of Hong Kong.

Dr Joseph Ting Sun-pao

Adjunct Professor; Honorary Senior Research Fellow,
Centre for Comparative and Public History, The Chinese University of Hong Kong

Former Chief Curator, Hong Kong Museum of History,
LCSD, HKSAR Government

Preface

As a city with one of the world's highest population densities, Hong Kong has faced numerous issues, transportation being one of the more serious. The transport system has been under strain because of intense city development, the building of new towns and stable economic growth. Compared with other cities around the world, the business environment in Hong Kong for bus services has been especially challenging.

The road capacity in urban areas in Hong Kong is limited, with relatively low private car ownership rate when set against other developed cities. As a result, most people commute by public transport. In areas which the train does not cover, the bus service is of great importance and is closely tied in with the lives of the people.

According to Transport Department statistics, the daily number of passenger trips on public transport in 2012, including the train, tram, bus, minibus, taxi and ferry, surpassed 11 million. Of that total 2.6 million passenger trips were recorded for KMB buses each day (the second most popular bus operator had 603,000). That means nearly 1 out of 4 people commuted by KMB on a daily basis.

As opposed to many other cities, bus travel is not recognised as a social service in Hong Kong and bus operators do not receive any direct subsidy from the government, except for the exemption from fuel tax. Providing services for a large number of passengers around the territory is therefore a tremendous undertaking for a privately-owned company such as KMB. It is also no easy task to keep its services at an exceptional standard.

Based on a wide range of information, this book explores the relationship between the development of the city and that of KMB – how a bus company with humble beginnings has overcome obstacles, big and small, to become a well-established operator with a huge fleet in Hong Kong.

Bus models and their technical development are not described in great detail here since there are already quite a number of such books written by experts. Through the selection of photos spanning different eras, I hope readers will be able to see the stunning changes that have happened in Hong Kong. I also hope the book will pique their interest in the development of our city and its transport system.

Ko Tim-keung

Kowloon Motor Bus Company purchased this bus manufactured by Leyland Motors in 1926. The bus route is displayed above the side windows. Photo taken outside Sham Shui Po Police Station.

NATHAN ROAD YAUMATI MONG KOK PRINCE EDWARD RD.
瑞蔴遮 油蔴地 旺角 太子路

THE KOWLOON MOTOR BUS Cº LTº

CHAPTER 01

DEVELOPMENT OF KOWLOON AND EARLY BUS SERVICES

Early Development of Kowloon

Most areas in the Kowloon Peninsula were not developed in the 1870s.

The development of the Kowloon Peninsula (the area south of Boundary Street and herein abbreviated as "Kowloon") was relatively slow after it was ceded to Britain in 1861 (the Convention of Peking was signed in the previous October). A large area of land was used by the British military to build army barracks and other defence facilities. Yau Ma Tei, Hung Hom and Tsim Sha Tsui were the first three districts to be developed in Kowloon.

Yau Ma Tei became the biggest market town in Kowloon within 10 years. Its population surged to over 8,000 in 1897 (the total population of Kowloon in 1891 was 14,200 only), making it Kowloon's biggest community. Thanks to the flourishing shipping business, the dockyards in Hung Hom grew dramatically, which in turn fuelled the development of the district. In the late 19th century, the population of Hung Hom reached 6,000, most of whom worked at the dockyards.

In addition, Hong Kong Wharf and Godown Co., founded by merchants Paul Chater and Kerfoot Hughes from Peninsular and Oriental Steam Navigation Company, was relocated from Wan Chai to Tsim Sha Tsui in 1875. The company was later renamed Hong Kong and Kowloon Wharf and Godown Co. Ltd. Following the building of a port, Tsim Sha Tsui gradually became an important location for international shipping.

In the 1880s, some private companies and organisations began small-scale land reclamation projects in Tsim Sha Tsui and Hung Hom. Similar projects had been tried first on Hong Kong Island and reclamation in Kowloon was more organised. Later, the government undertook reclamation projects on a bigger scale in Yau Ma Tei and Tai Kok Tsui. The expansive piece of land to the west of Kowloon facilitated systematic urban planning and the construction of roads.

The New Territories was leased to Britain in 1898. As land stretched north to Shenzhen River, east to Mirs Bay and west to Deep Bay, the total area of Hong Kong increased 10-fold. This would benefit the overall development of Hong Kong. Construction of the Kowloon-Canton Railway (British Section) was given the green light after the New Territories was leased to Britain. In a bid to extend the train to the southern part of the Kowloon Peninsula, Governor Matthew Nathan (whose tenure ran from 1904 to 1907) decided to reclaim more land in Tsim Sha Tsui and open Chatham Road, as well as Salisbury Road, on the reclaimed land.

Governor Nathan had great confidence in the development of Kowloon and the New Territories. Starting from 1906, the government gradually opened many roads in these two areas. Three of the roads built earliest were Nathan Road, Canton Road and Shanghai Street South. These major roads were later linked with others, becoming Kowloon's chief route network which would eventually be covered by the main routes operated by The Kowloon Motor Bus Co. (1933) Ltd.

Yau Ma Tei waterfront around 1880. Yau Ma Tei waterfront became Kowloon's largest community in less than 20 years.

Villagers building roads in the early 20th century.

The Kowloon-Canton Railway (British Section) opened in 1910 (the terminus building in Tsim Sha Tsui was completed and opened in 1916) and in turn helped road development in Kowloon. In 1916, the main sections of the New Territories Ring Road were finished. The 56-mile long route is actually a loop from Tsim Sha Tsui Ferry Pier to Salisbury Road, encompassing Tai Po, Fanling, Sheung Shui, Au Tau, Ping Shan, Castle Peak, Tsuen Wan, Lai Chi Kok and Nathan Road.

The expansion of roads laid a solid foundation for the growth of public transport, particularly that of bus services. To accommodate an increasing number of vehicles on the roads, the government executed plans to expand the network, improve road surface hardness as well as malleability, and reduce winding roads as well as slope steepness. As a result, the slopes in Kowloon and the New Territories are less steep than those on Hong Kong Island. For example, the steepest slope ratio (from Sham Shui Po to Tai Po Road in Sha Tin) is just 1:17. On September 21, 1922, in a Legislative Council meeting that was to approve the allocation of $45,000 to improve the roads from Fanling to Yuen Long, Claud Severn, the Chairman of the Council, suggested the prerequisite for public bus services should be a comprehensive road network.

Reclamation work began in the Sham Shui Po area in Western Kowloon in 1902. After 10 or so years, it became a new commercial and residential area for Chinese people. In 1916, another reclamation project commenced in Kowloon Bay in East Kowloon – the biggest project since Hong Kong was ceded to Britain. It was spearheaded by Chinese merchants such as Sir Ho Kai and Mr Au Tak and, from when it was in the planning stages, the project took into account factors such as the living environment and hygiene conditions, as well as road and sea transport. The aim was to build a modern Chinese community that would be able to accommodate 4,000 to 6,000 flats on 230 hectares of land. It was hoped that the community would appeal to better-off local residents and overseas Chinese, as well as Chinese who arrived in Hong Kong after the 1911 Revolution.

The rapid development of Kowloon as shown in this photo taken in around 1910.

Ma Tau Wai area around 1920. The tracks shown in the photo were used to transport sandstone for land reclamation in Kowloon Bay. On the right is Kowloon City Road. The building on the hill is Holy Trinity Church.

The rent in areas like Sham Shui Po and Kowloon City was relatively low since new buildings were sprouting. Consequently, many manufacturers set up factories there. These small factories facilitated local industrial growth and also created job opportunities, resulting in lots of workers residing in these areas. From the 1920s, several new roads were built and old ones expanded, including Waterloo Road, Prince Edward Road, Argyle Street and Boundary Street. Meanwhile, garden villas were established in areas such as Ho Man Tin, Kowloon Tong, Kowloon Tsai (the Yau Yat Chuen area) and Kadoorie Hill. Quite a large number of organisations, including banks, hotels and all kinds of industrial facilities, were set up in Kowloon. Christian groups and their affiliated organisations helped these areas thrive as well, since they built churches and schools.

Dubbed as "guardian of Kowloon's interests", Portuguese Legislative Councillor J.P. Braga (Braga Circuit in Kadoorie Hill is named after him) was always concerned about Kowloon's development. In a Legislative Council meeting in 1932, he described Kowloon as a piece of "promised land".

Early Bus Services

When did public bus services first appear in Hong Kong? According to archival records, they can be traced to 1909, when buses ran between Tsim Sha Tsui Ferry Pier and the dockyard in Hung Hom. In Notification No. 449 of the Government Gazette, public transport regulations stated that the fare for each passenger was 10 cents under the section "Fare for Public Motor-Cars in British Kowloon". It also stated that "if appropriated by less than 3 passengers, per passenger, 30 cents." However, no further information has been found to give a full picture of early bus services, including the company, number of passengers, bus types or operating hours.

In 1920, a group of European residents set up Kowloon Residents' Association which was aimed at protecting and improving the living environment in Kowloon. The Association proposed that the government consider setting up bus services that would link Kai Tak Bund (the residential area of Kowloon Bay's reclamation project) and other Kowloon districts after the completion of several thousand residential buildings on the reclaimed land in Kowloon Bay. In a meeting on November 18, the Legislative Council discussed the proposal of operating bus services in Kowloon. It pointed out that the overhaul of roads should be finished as soon as possible in order to advance transport development (mainly bus services). Some legislators even suggested that the government should establish bus services to assist the growth of Kai Tak Bund.

In 1921, the Attorney General proposed an amendment to the "Vehicles and Traffic Regulation Ordinance, 1912" on the grounds that the government would soon provide franchised bus services in Kowloon and the New Territories. The reasons stated by the government were as follows:

The photo shows Ma Tau Chung and To Kwa Wan viewed from Pak Hok Shan in Kowloon City in 1926. In the distance is the newly-constructed Argyle Street and in the foreground are the stone walls of Kowloon Walled City.

Kai Tak Bund in 1927, when the land reclamation of Kowloon Bay was handed over to the government. The open space at the bottom of the photo is a Royal Air Force base.

1. To ensure a service to certain outlying districts which would not be served under a system of free competition.

2. To ensure a proper service during the slacker times of the day.

3. To enable the Government, by control of vehicles, fares and other aspects, to secure a better service for the public.

4. To prevent racing, arising from one competitor trying to undercut another.

5. To prevent the use of unroadworthy vehicles.

In April 1921, the government advertised in the gazette and invited contractors to bid for bus services in Kowloon. Some of the technical requirements were as follows:

1. Not to exceed 20 feet in length, 7 feet 2 inches in width and 10 feet in height.

2. 19 adult persons including the driver and conductor.

3. 2 ¼ tons when unloaded.

4. Capacity 15 miles (approximately 24 km) per hour fully loaded on level ground.

5. Sufficient to take the motor vehicle when fully loaded up an incline of 1 in 15 for a length of ¼ mile.

An overturned bus on Kowloon City Road in Ma Tau Chung in 1923. Back then, some roads in Kowloon were still very narrow.

Only 4 routes were proposed, as follows:

Route No.	Details	Operating hours	Maximum fare (pay by section)	
			First-class	Second-class
1.	Kowloon Ferry (Tsim Sha Tsui) to Sham Shui Po (Alternate bus via Ho Man Tin)	07:00 – 23:30 Every 10 minutes	5-15 cents	2-6 cents
2.	Hung Hom to Kowloon Ferry (Tsim Sha Tsui)	07:00 – 23:30 Every 10 minutes	5-10 cents	2-4 cents
3.	Hung Hom to Sham Shui Po (Alternate bus via Ho Man Tin)	06:35 – 00:05 Every 10 minutes	5-15 cents	2-6 cents
4.	Hung Hom to Kowloon City	06:35 – 00:15 Every 30 minutes	5-10 cents	2-4 cents

The proposed technical criteria might have been too strict since none of the bidding contractors were able to meet them, leading the government to recall the franchised bus routes. The following companies then ran bus services in Kowloon and the New Territories until 1933:

1. Kowloon Motor Bus Company operated 9 Ford buses with primary routes between Tsim Sha Tsui Ferry Pier and Sham Shui Po from 1921. It also ran secondary routes between Nathan Road and Hung Hom.

2. Nam Hing Bus Company operated 4 lorry-converted buses and provided services between Yuen Long and Sheung Shui from 1921.

3. Kai Tack Motor Bus Company operated 20 lorry-converted buses in Kowloon from 1923.

4. China Motor Bus Company operated 15 lorry-converted buses in Kowloon from 1924.

5. Hong Kong and Cowloon (sic) Taxicab Company operated both taxi and bus services.

6. Cheung Mei Bus Company operated 6 lorry-converted buses in the New Territories in 1925.

7. Chun Hing Motor Bus & Company operated bus services to beaches at weekends in the 1920s.

8. Hongkong, Kowloon & New Territory Motor-Bus and Transport Company (details of services not known).

9. Liang Kwong Motor Bus Company closed in 1932 (details of services not known).

According to the Hong Kong Daily Press report published on November 18, 1921, Kowloon Motor Bus Company officially commenced business after Christmas that year. It operated 9 small Ford buses with a capacity of 16 (including the driver and conductor). There was a driver's compartment at the head of the bus and the driver's seat was conjoined with a two-passenger seat, separated by a partition. Behind the driver's compartment were three rows of passenger seats. Each row accommodated 4 passengers and the seats were divided into first-class and second-class. The number of first-class and second-class seats would vary, depending on the demand. The top of the bus was made of wood and the sides, as well as the tail, were open. Waterproof curtains could be drawn on rainy days. However, the bus compartment was far too high off the ground and sparked controversy since it was difficult for women to board the vehicle. Female passengers had to step on a stool which was 20 inches high and climb a further 18 inches to get on the bus. Newspapers joked that women in skirts need to practise climbing stools at home.

VIEW OF THE MANUFACTORY "THE ORIENT"
From NATHAN ROAD MONGKOK·KOWLOON (HONG-KONG.)

The government once considered setting up tram services in Kowloon. Trams can be seen on this promotional leaflet of Orient Tobacco Manufactory of Hong Kong on Nathan Road (between Shantung Street and Dundas Street).

Hong Kong went through some turbulent times as far as politics and the economy were concerned. Seamen went on strike in 1922 and the General Strike broke out in 1925. The General Strike lasted 16 months and dealt a heavy blow to Hong Kong, paralysing its production and transport. Trade almost came to a standstill and quite a number of companies had to close down. Government revenue also dropped drastically. The business of bus companies inevitably suffered under the circumstances. Hongkong, Kowloon & New Territory Motor-Bus and Transport Company filed for bankruptcy in July 1926 (see liquidation notice opposite), while Kai Tack Motor Bus Company followed suit in September 1926.

Nevertheless, the government was still determined to develop Kowloon and even proposed the setting up of tram services in the territory in 1923. In a meeting on October 4, the Legislative Council approved a grant of $10,000 for such services (how the grant would be used was not stated in the minutes). In view of London's experience, the government realised that buses would allow greater flexibility and produce less noise than trams. Trams would also get in the way of other vehicles. Consequently, the government vetoed the proposal to operate trams in Kowloon. With a nod to the fact that trams were gradually being replaced in other big cities, the proposal was then dropped altogether.

A few months later, at the Legislative Council on March 13, 1924, Legislator H. E. Pollock, K.C., raised questions about bus services. The government said that it would offer franchised bus services once the conditions were right. At the same meeting, when asked by Pollock whether the bus company had to originate in the UK and the tyres also had to be manufactured there, the government did not hesitate to reply in the affirmative.

In 1926, however, the government's stance towards franchised bus services changed again. At the Legislative Council meeting on November 4, Colonial Secretary W. T. Southorn, reiterating that transport services were conducive to the development of Kowloon, said that trams, with or without tracks, were inferior to buses and that bus services in Kowloon should be run by private enterprise. He said, "The Government considers that the traffic problem in Kowloon can best be solved by bus services run by private enterprise and is not in favour of the creation of any monopoly... it is in favour of open competition for road transport in Kowloon as being most likely to meet economically and efficiently the needs of the local population."

The government's second dropping of its franchised bus services proposal was probably due to the dire situation at the time. The General Strike had just ended and the business environment was bleak, with some operators having trouble maintaining their existing bus services. Franchising bus services might have discouraged contractors, and the Colonial Secretary might have recalled the proposal in order to pacify them.

In September 1932, aware of the lack of planned bus services, the government once again invited bids for Hong Kong-wide

In the Matter of the Companies Ordinances 1911-1925,
and
In the Matter of the Hongkong, Kowloon & New Territory Motor-Bus and Transport Company, Limited.

(IN LIQUIDATION)

NOTICE is hereby given, in pursuance of Section 188 of the Companies Ordinance, 1911, that a General Meeting of the members of the above-named Company will be held at the Offices of M. Y. San & Company, Limited, No. 98, Queen's Road Central, on Monday, the 9th day of August, 1926, at 3 o'clock p.m. for the purpose of having an account laid before them, showing the manner in which the winding-up has been conducted and the property of the Company disposed of, and of hearing any explanation that may be given by the liquidator, and also of determining by Extraordinary Resolution the manner in which the books, accounts and documents of the Company and of the Liquidator thereof, shall disposed.

Dated the 8th day of July, 1926.

LAU YUK WAN,
Liquidator.

A company liquidation notice in the Government Gazette of 1926.

Part of the bus fleet of Kai Tack Motor Bus Company in 1926. The company had already been bought by Hong Kong Tramways.

The bus terminal in front of Tsim Sha Tsui Ferry Pier around 1923. The buses in the photo belonged to Kowloon Motor Bus Company and Kai Tack Motor Bus Company respectively. Most of these buses were manufactured by Ford in the USA.

franchised bus services in the Government Gazette. The tender stated that the company who won the bid would operate the bus services of the whole city, or two companies would operate separately on Hong Kong Island and in Kowloon (including the New Territories).

A number of points in the 17-page tender are worth noting:

1. The licence or licences would be for a period or term of 15 years commencing on the 11th day of June, 1933.

2. The service or services should be conducted only by means of vehicles of British manufacture, with the exception of any vehicle of non-British manufacture which was owned by the successful tenderer and was in use by him immediately before the 11th June, 1933.

3. The Governor in Council would not approve of the use of double-deck vehicles on roads on Hong Kong Island. Approval of the use of such vehicles on any road in Kowloon would be subject to the advice of the Director of Public Works as to the suitability of the roads.

4. The Inspector General of Police and any officer authorised in writing by him were responsible for inspecting motor vehicles and works connected with the service. (The transport department had not yet been set up.)

5. The licensee should keep records in respect of every aspect of its service, including: number of motor vehicles running; number of daily journeys and mileage recorded by each vehicle; number of passengers carried by each vehicle on each journey; details of receipts in respect of each section and route.

6. A deposit as security of compliance should be lodged by the licensee with the Colonial Treasurer by the successful tenderer. The amount of the deposit should be, in the case of a service for the whole of Hong Kong, $50,000; for the whole of the Island of Hong Kong, $20,000; for the whole of the Kowloon Peninsula, including the New Territories, $30,000.

7. No tender would be accepted unless the tenderer stated, if an individual, that he was a British subject and, if a firm or company, that the management and the administrative staff or an effective majority thereof, to the satisfaction of the Governor in Council, were or would be British subjects; and that the control would be within Hong Kong and essentially British.

8. In the event of any special emergency, the Governor in Council might direct that the Hong Kong Government would take over the service.

9. British servicemen (in uniform) and children below the age of 12 years would be carried 1st class at 2nd class rates (if available). Police officers and postmen on duty would be carried free of charge.

The tender listed the bus routes in Kowloon and the New Territories, timetable, fare and maximum passenger capacity (Appendix 1). There would be no designated bus stops and passengers would be able to get off anywhere. The routes covered areas with a high population density and places where the economy was growing.

In 1935, to celebrate the 25th anniversary of the coronation of King George V, the headquarters of KMB in Mong Kok were adorned with lights.

CHAPTER 02

BEGINNING OF FRANCHISED BUS SERVICES

The Kowloon Motor Bus Company (1933) Limited

Mr Lui Chung Yuen once served as General Manager of KMB and he is the grandson of Mr Lui Leung, one of the major shareholders and founders of KMB. He remembers that his grandfather and his fellow Taishan townsman, Mr William Louey Sui Tak, intended to bid for the franchised bus services in Kowloon and the New Territories. To increase their chances of winning, they teamed up with Mr Tang Shiu Kin, Mr Tam Woon Tong and Mr Lam Ming Fan, all members of the social elite. In the end, they won the bid.

The franchised bus services on Hong Kong Island were awarded to China Motor Bus Company. In May 1933, Kowloon Motor Bus Company was restructured and re-registered as The Kowloon Motor Bus Company (1933) Limited (KMB). Mr Tang Shiu Kin was the first Chairman of the Board and later became Director. He was in office for half a decade. Mr Chau Sik Nin, Mr Woo Pak Chuen, Mr Chung Sze Yuen and Dr Norman Leung have succeeded him as Chairman.

On June 11, 1933, KMB officially took over 11 routes in Kowloon and the New Territories previously operated by other companies to add to the 7 it already ran, giving it a total of 18 routes. Prior to that, it had bought 35 buses from China Motor Bus Company and 26 from Kai Tack Motor Bus Company through the government. According to a report in Kung Sheung Daily of June 9, 1933, the number of KMB buses rose to 110. As some of its vehicles had been purchased from other companies, the different bus types posed certain maintenance problems, causing KMB to retire some buses and buy new ones to bring the fleet up to strength. Kai Tack Motor Bus Company, once a major bus operator, was duly dissolved in July 1933.

After gaining the franchise for bus services in Kowloon and the New Territories, KMB had to operate the routes mandated in the tender. Many of these routes covered the dockyards in the Hung Hom area, reflecting the large number of dock workers at the time.

The busy bus terminal at Tsim Sha Tsui Ferry Pier in the 1930s.

Main routes operated by KMB and their fares:

Route	First-class	Second-class
Tsim Sha Tsui to Austin Road	10 cents	–
Tsim Sha Tsui to Kowloon Dockyard/Sham Shui Po/Prince Edward Road Junction	10 cents	5 cents
Tsim Sha Tsui to Kowloon City/Ngau Chi Wan/Lai Chi Kok	15 cents	10 cents
Austin Road to Kowloon Dockyard	10 cents	5 cents
Austin Road to Ma Tau Kok Road/Kowloon City	15 cents	10 cents
Pak Hoi Street to Sham Shui Po/Kowloon City	15 cents	10 cents
Pak Hoi Stret to Ngau Chi Wan/Lai Chi Kok	20 cents	10 cents
Kowloon Dockyard to Kowloon City	15 cents	10 cents
Waterloo Road to Ngau Chi Wan	15 cents	10 cents
Kowloon City to Ngau Chi Wan	10 cents	5 cents
Yen Chow Street to Lai Chi Kok	15 cents	10 cents
Yaumatei Ferry Pier to Kowloon Dockyard/Sham Shui Po/Kowloon City	15 cents	10 cents
Yaumatei Ferry Pier to Ngau Chi Wan/Kowloon City/Lai Chi Kok	20 cents	10 cents
To Kwa Wan to Yaumatei Ferry Pier	15 cents	10 cents
To Kwa Wan to Sham Shui Po	20 cents	10 cents
Mong Kok to Yuen Long	70 cents	50 cents
Mong Kok to Castle Peak	60 cents	40 cents
Mong Kok to Tai Lam Chung	55 cents	35 cents
Mong Kok to Tsing Lung Tau	45 cents	30 cents
Mong Kok to Ting Kau	40 cents	25 cents
Mong Kok to Tsuen Wan	30 cents	20 cents
Sheung Shui to Tsung Pak Long	–	5 cents
Sheung Shui to Kam Tin	–	10 cents
Sheung Shui to Lok Ma Chau/San Tin	–	20 cents
Sheung Shui to Mai Po	–	25 cents

A Route 10 KMB bus on Prince Edward Road in the mid-1930s.
St. Teresa's Church is on the left.

Sheung Shui to Fung Kat Heung	-	30 cents
Sheung Shui to Au Tau	-	35 cents
Sheung Shui to Yuen Long	-	40 cents
Fanling to Lung Yeuk Tau	-	50 cents
Fanling to Kwan Tei	-	10 cents
Fanling to Sha Tau Kok	-	30 cents
Fanling to Tai Po Hui	-	15 cents
Kam Tin to Yuen Long	-	5 cents

Source: *Hong Kong Yearbook 1934*

Tall trees lined both sides near the Jordan Road section of Nathan Road in 1935. Such trees were the reason double-deck buses were not approved at the time.

Even after KMB gained the franchise for bus services in Kowloon and the New Territories, it still faced competition from other transport operators. The 1934 Hong Kong Yearbook described public transport as follows: "The transport system in Hong Kong has grown dramatically in recent years. We have seen the expansion of long-distance bus services. We also have taxis and illegally operated vehicles. They are cheap and fast and thus many people choose to use them." It can therefore be seen that KMB did not monopolise public transport in the areas of its operations. At the same time, with the growth of bus services, rickshaws, previously another major mode of transport, were gradually eliminated. Within a year of the government's approval of franchised bus services, several hundred rickshaws were no longer in use. The 1934 Hong Kong Yearbook predicted that rickshaws would be obsolete in a few years. However, their prediction was inaccurate, as rickshaws were still operating more than 30 years later!

Meeting the requirements laid down for franchised bus services was far from easy for KMB. Four months into its operations, the company was taken to court and fined because it failed to run in accordance with the timetable. Reports surfaced that the company was planning to run evening classes for its employees. The classes would cover different areas, such as rules of the road, mechanics, first aid and even work etiquette. The Company Secretary saw such training as urgent and it was apparent that the company was proactive in its desire to improve its services.

The first depot of KMB (bottom right-hand corner) located at the junction of Nathan Road and Bute Street. In the distance is Lai Chi Kok Road.

The government tender of 1932 stated that double-deck buses would be allowed to operate in Kowloon if the Director of Public Works approved them. According to a news report in 1938, KMB planned to undertake a trial operation of double-deck buses on Route 1, which carried the most passengers at the time. The news report also pointed out that double-deck buses were convenient and embraced by a number of major cities around the world. In fact, the company had already purchased 3 to 4 double-deck buses from Europe (meaning the UK). The report stated that if the trial went smoothly, the bus operator would introduce more double-deck buses in Kowloon. In the end, the proposal was not implemented since the tall trees lining both sides of Nathan Road obstructed the operation of such buses. Since the late 19th century, the government had put great emphasis on the greening of urban areas, particularly along roads, setting up in 1872 a specific department to plant trees in the city. Some travel articles actually said that tourists were impressed with the big trees on both sides of the roads, which gave them a good impression of Hong Kong. If KMB was going to operate double-deck buses on Nathan Road and other major routes, many trees would have to be chopped down and this was not acceptable to the government. As a result, double-deck buses did not make it onto the roads before the Japanese Occupation of Hong Kong in 1941.

Industrial growth in Kowloon

The steady development of bus services in Kowloon in the 1930s was closely related to population as well as industrial growth.

After the General Strike that took place between 1925 and 1926, Hong Kong's economy slowly recovered. However, in 1929, there was a global recession, which hit international trade as the economic development of many countries and regions experienced catastrophic setbacks. In this period, owing to Hong Kong's social stability, it continued to play an important role in international trade. Thanks to a well established network, its industrial products were successfully exported to other parts of the world, particularly South East Asia. Meanwhile, overseas Chinese came to Hong Kong to invest. All in all, the global recession did not have such an impact on Hong Kong as it had on other regions.

In the 1930s, Japanese militarism started to rise in China. The Mukden Incident occurred in 1931 and there was also the Shanghai Incident on January 28, 1932. To maintain Hong Kong's development at a time of such uncertainty, the UK offered trade incentives and lower tariffs. Products manufactured in Hong Kong were exempt from the 10% import tax if they were shipped to the UK and its sovereign territories. Many merchants seized the opportunity and built factories in Hong Kong. These factories were low-tech and export-oriented, manufacturing items such as cotton cloth and cotton products, metal products, torches, batteries, porcelain products, rubber shoes and cans. Many of these newly-built factories were situated in areas such as Sham Shui Po, Tai Kok Tsui, Mong Kok, Yau Ma Tei, To Kwa Wan and Kowloon City, while a small number of factories were located in the New Territories. At a Legislative Council meeting in September 1934, some legislators remarked that Hong Kong's most important industrial facilities were located on the Kowloon Peninsula. In the years that followed, the industrial sector in Kowloon was to develop further.

In 1934, the Chinese Manufacturers' Association of Hong Kong was established and in 1938 it launched the Products Expo (later known as Hong Kong Brands and Products Expo). The Expo aimed to promote products made in Hong Kong

A factory in Sham Shui Po before World War II. Factories like this one flourished in the 1930s, contributing to the growth of Kowloon.

and marketed them as being as good as those manufactured in China, hence appealing to the Mainland and overseas Chinese markets. Later, as the threat of a war posed by Japanese militarism grew greater, a growing number of factories in Mainland China moved south to Hong Kong on account of its relative stability.

An increase in job opportunities led to population growth. In 1934, there were around 300,000 Chinese living in Kowloon (including new Kowloon, which was north of Boundary Street and south of Lion Rock; that is the area encompassing today's Kwun Tong, Wong Tai Sin, Kowloon City and Kowloon Tong). Three years later, the number rose to 340,000. This increase of over 10% showed that Kowloon was thriving. What distinguished Kowloon from Hong Kong Island was that there were no trams operating there and buses thus became the major mode of transport, linking districts in Kowloon and those in the New Territories. Demand for bus services was rising continuously.

Japanese propaganda postcard at the beginning of the Japanese Occupation. It shows 3 buses on Nathan Road and the hustle and bustle of Hong Kong. Nathan Road was renamed Katori Dori.

CHAPTER 03

WORLD WAR II AND KOWLOON BUS SERVICES

Gloom brought by the war

In 1937, total war between China and Japan began. Tens of thousands of refugees from the southern part of China and coastal cities fled to Hong Kong. In 1941, the population of Hong Kong exceeded 1.5 million and was about 1.8 million according to some records. To accommodate the large number of refugees, the government built many large refugee camps in urban areas and the New Territories. In Kowloon, camps were built in King's Park, Ma Tau Chung, Kowloon Tsai, Ngau Tau Kok, etc. The biggest refugee camp in the New Territories was located in Kam Tin - Pat Heung (the land was originally reserved for a small-scale military aerodrome which later became Shek Kong Airfield). Nevertheless, the facilities were far from adequate for the refugees, many of whom were forced to live on the streets or even in the countryside. The population surge disrupted public services, including bus services.

Starting from 1938, complaints about insufficient bus services were occasionally reported in the newspapers, as here (see clipping on p.45):

"Route 11, operated by KMB, runs between Lai Chi Kok and Kowloon City, via Hung Hom. Lately, it has become unusually crowded and is often fully loaded. The maximum standing capacity is frequently reached. To avoid being fined, the conductor often requires passengers to leave the bus. Many mainland refugees who have fled to Hong Kong live in the Lai Chi Kok and Cheung Sha Wan area. Therefore the number of passengers who commute from Lai Chi Kok to Yau Ma Tei has risen. There is an urgent need for more frequent bus services on this route. Current bus services are insufficient. When a bus is fully loaded, the conductor has to turn away passengers who come late, resulting in delays. It is hoped that KMB will address this issue..."

Refugees came to Hong Kong for relief in 1941.

Refugee camps in the Kowloon area in 1939.

In addition to the population surge, half-price public transport fares offered to some refugees led to an increase in passengers. This measure was undoubtedly good news for the refugees. However, the number of buses remained the same and services were thus adversely affected. There were 136 buses operating in Kowloon and the New Territories as of 1939, just 26 more than the number in 1933 when the bus company first gained the franchise for bus services.

In 1941, the situation worsened and the Kowloon Residents' Association frequently met with KMB, lobbying for increased service frequencies. The bus operator responded by saying that war had broken out in Europe and the UK was in the midst of a struggle with Germany and therefore unable to manufacture buses for Hong Kong. Even if they were able to do so, shipping buses from Europe to Hong Kong was no easy matter in wartime. There was little KMB could do, even though it did want to improve its services. At the beginning of 1941, to resolve the dilemma, the bus operator proposed to the government that it purchase buses from the US temporarily. However, the proposal was not approved and another plan to operate double-deck buses on main routes was also turned down (double-deck buses did not need to be imported from the UK directly - they could be modified from single-deck buses). In short, before the Japanese military occupied Hong Kong, KMB was unable to improve its bus services as a result of the shortage of vehicles caused by the war in Europe.

九龍居民對

九龍汽車公司兩點希望

增加十一號綫車輛行走
改良新用巴士以策萬全

中華巴士公司亦宜改善四號綫車輛

（本報專訪）九龍汽車公司第十一號綫、為行走荔枝角經紅磡至九龍城、此綫搭客、日來異常擁擠、由是來往巴士、常苦滿座、即催企立名額、亦常擠出、為防警察盤問起見、售票員惟將過額搭客勸令落車、查此十一號綫、為新設者、在未設立前、係由十二號路綫之車行走、（由深水埗往九龍城）蓋從前此綫、甚少搭客、故此綫車輛、特慶蔚本、從而九龍公司、亦用小型之車輛行走、開行次數、亦甚稀疏、即自改變後（由荔枝角經紅磡至九龍城）、所用車輛、一仍如舊、而開行班次、亦未有增加、復此路綫為最長、從前與在荔枝角及長沙灘一帶居住者甚少、所以往來搭客、亦甚稀疏、除在天熟之外、亦豪無幾、但自內地難民逃來港後、因歡居荔枝角及長沙灘一帶、日漸眾多、由是從荔枝角出油麻地之搭客、飲巴增多、同時田狂角與油藏地而入九龍城者、亦須乘搭此路巴士、從此可見此綫車輛、為便利搭客往來與安全計、實有增加車輛行走之必要、蓋在目前情況、車輛俠應既少、歡叉不見增多、搭客滿座時、後至者、輕將傳票員拒絕登車、因而阻談公事不少、一般居民對于九龍汽車公司所用新款巴士、即由車房之中央上落之一種、甚表不滿、第一點、因此種車身較、每在停止處開駛時、進退急劇、常使搭客傾倒車上、良蔚車身位稍不穩偄、偶於于地、必易發生危險、關於此點、希望該車公司、速關改善、以策萬全云、至如中華巴士公司、對于行走四號路綫車輛、次數既少、而晚上收車復早、因此、對于居民來往、殊感不便、僑公私利益計、甚望該公司有以改善云。

Bus services in Kowloon during the Japanese Occupation

From 1938, the international state of affairs deteriorated, becoming extremely tense. The government and military started to enact protection measures against the chance of war. One such measure was setting up Air Raid Precautions (ARP), which provided air defence training for government officials and employees of public services. Another was to work out a contingency plan to convert buses into ambulances during the war. In 1939, 250 employees of KMB and the Hongkong and Kowloon Wharf and Godown Company undertook war drills, including rescue and destruction exercises. The exercises were aimed at preventing goods and materials, like buses, from falling into enemy hands if Kowloon was lost to the Japanese.

On December 8, 1941, the Japanese military launched an attack on the US naval base at Pearl Harbor (December 7 in the US). On the same day, it launched an assault on Hong Kong, marking the beginning of a full-blown war. In the morning, the Japanese military conducted air raids on Kai Tak Aerodrome and the army barracks in Sham Shui Po (now the area of Sham Shui Po Park and Lai Kok Estate). Since the government was not able to release sufficient information and many air raid exercises had taken place before, many of the city's residents were not aware that the Japanese had begun their invasion of the New Territories. Buses were still running in the morning. Passengers from Kowloon City and Sham Shui Po delivered the news that Kai Tak and Sham Shui Po Barracks were under attack. Bus services in Kowloon and the New Territories were finally halted in the afternoon. On the afternoon of the 11th, the Commander of the British Garrison in Hong Kong ordered the withdrawal of troops from Kowloon. In the early morning of the 13th, the last troops guarding Devil's Peak crossed Lei Yue Mun and retreated to Hong Kong Island. Kowloon thus fell into the hands of the Japanese.

Japanese troops assemble on Nathan Road in Mong Kok before launching a full-blown attack on Kowloon. An abandoned bus can be seen at the back.

Japanese troops march to Mong Kok via Tai Po Road during the invasion. There are many abandoned buses along the road.

On Christmas Day, Hong Kong was already fighting a losing battle. After 17 days of fierce fighting against the overwhelming Japanese forces, the Governor, Sir Mark Young formally surrendered the British Crown Colony of Hong Kong to Imperial Japan. The Japanese Occupation of Hong Kong had begun. Bus services in Kowloon could not operate normally from the start of the Japanese Occupation since some vehicles were destroyed and others were taken over by the Japanese army. Some of these were converted into lorries while others had their engines removed for other purposes. The Japanese also transported a number of buses to southern China for other uses. Only a few buses resumed service at the beginning of 1942.

In light of the public's needs and calls from the Japanese, in October 1942, a transport company named Hong Kong Motor Transport Co. was authorised by the Japanese and established to offer transport in Hong Kong. The company was founded and funded by a group of local merchants. It was not related to any of the bus companies that operated before the war. During the Occupation, only 4 routes were operated by Hong Kong Motor Transport Co.: from Tsim Sha Tsui (the Japanese renamed it Minato-ku) to Sham Shui Po (Aoyama-ku); from Tsim Sha Tsui to Kowloon City (Moto-ku); from Tsim Sha Tsui to Lai Chi Kok (via Chatham Road); from Tsim Sha Tsui to Lai Chi Kok (via Katori Dori, which refers to Nathan Road, then turning into Waterloo Road). Fares ranged from 10 to 20 sen (sub-units of the Japanese yen currency). There were only 2 routes in the New Territories: from Shenzhen to Sha Tau Kok and from Mong Kok (Daikaku-ku) to Sheung Shui, with the maximum fare at 35 sen. These services never met actual demand because there were only around 50 buses running in total, less than half of the service before the war.

The insufficiency of bus services led to horse-drawn carriage services appearing in 1942. These operated on 4 routes, carrying passengers around districts such as Tsim Sha Tsui, Hung Hom, Kowloon City, Lai Chi Kok and Kowloon Tong. Fares ranged from 10 to 40 sen. The horse-drawn carriages also carried freight and were a common sight during the Japanese Occupation. Workers were hired to pick up horse manure along the routes. As a newspaper reported:

"Rubber tyres were used and there was a canopy that protected passengers from rain and wind. The carriage accommodated a maximum number of 15 passengers and no standing was allowed. There were lights at the back for communication with the transport police. The carriage was also equipped with an emergency exit door. The groom's seat was in the front and had space for two people. Two horses pulled the carriage. The ride was quite stable and it was an interesting experience. "

As there were not enough horses, the carriage company had to borrow some from Keibakai (Jockey Club). Towards the end of the Occupation, Keibakai also ran short of horses, meaning that the carriage company had to close down. In fact, during the Occupation, when resources were extremely scarce, most Kowloon residents went to their destinations on foot.

Recovery period

On August 15, 1945, Japan surrendered. On August 30, British Rear Admiral (later Sir) Cecil Harcourt sailed into Hong Kong on board the cruiser HMS Swiftsure to re-establish the British government's control over the colony. He became the de facto governor of Hong Kong as commander-in-chief and head of the military administration.

According to a report of the military government, many roads in Hong Kong were still in good condition, but those in urban areas and the New Territories needed repair. Because of a lack of maintenance during the Japanese Occupation, many buses were so worn out that they could not be operated anymore. Notwithstanding this, the military government asked KMB to resume its services soon after it was established. Some former KMB employees immediately went back to work and it did not take them long to locate a small number of buses parked at the sports ground at Boundary Street. However, only 6 buses could still be used, 2 of which met the minimum safety requirements. These 2 buses carried passengers in Kowloon between Tsim Sha Tsui Ferry Pier and St. Teresa's Church on Prince Edward Road. Ten days later, the remaining 4 buses resumed service after undergoing repairs.

Besides the lack of buses, there was a shortage of parts, particularly tyres. To meet the shortfall, a small number of lorries were converted into buses, although the supply was still unable to meet the demand. To alleviate the problem, the Royal Air Force dispatched some of its vehicles as public buses. In May 1946, former Governor Sir Mark Young returned to Hong Kong and resumed his duties, marking the end of military administration and the return of civilian rule to Hong Kong.

A bus at the junction of Prince Edward Road and Boundary Street in Kowloon City in late 1945. The building with the domed roof is La Salle College.

Hong Kong's economy gradually recovered during the first half of 1946. By the end of the year, thanks to civilian rule, the recovery had really kicked in. In 1949, Hong Kong regained its position as a major port of export to Europe and America. Meanwhile, the population grew dramatically, from 600,000 shortly after the war to 1.8 million in 1947, exceeding the number before the war commenced. This boosted the workforce, providing ample human resources for the economy. At the same time, the population surge led to social concerns in areas such as employment, food, medicine, housing and transport.

To deal with the influx of passengers, KMB once again proposed operating double-deck buses. During the war, many trees lining Nathan Road had been cut down as a result of fuel shortages during the Japanese Occupation, sometimes at the expense of the lives of those who attempted chupping down the trunks of these trees. Except for the Whitfield Barracks section of Nathan Road, very few trees were left, which meant that the government no longer opposed plans for the use of double-deck buses.

At the end of 1948, KMB purchased Daimler A double-deck buses from the UK. In the following April, 4 Daimler As commenced operations on Route 1, running between Tsim Sha Tsui and Kowloon City. By 1950, KMB had bought a total of 75 double-deckers out of a total fleet of around 200 buses. In just two years, double-deck buses had become a common sight in Kowloon.

Yau Ma Tei section of Nathan Road in 1949. Double-deck buses were used in Kowloon, starting from that year. The bottom right-hand corner of the photo shows a lorry-converted bus. The white building is the Alhambra Theatre.

After the Japanese military surrendered in 1945, KMB quickly converted lorries into buses to resume bus services.

Chuk Yuen Bus Terminus in Wong Tai Sin in the mid-1970s

CHAPTER 04

BEGINNINGS OF AN INDUSTRIAL CITY

Rapid growth of the industrial sector

Hong Kong's trade activities recovered after the war and, by, 1947, economic activity was even stronger than before the conflict. The Korean War broke out in 1950 and the UN, supported by the US, imposed an embargo on China, dealing a heavy blow to Hong Kong's transit trade. An influx of Mainland Chinese provided cheap labour for Hong Kong. More importantly, manufacturers, including textile factories from Shanghai and Jiangsu, as well as Zhejiang, brought with them technology and money. They originally purchased machinery from the US, UK and other western countries. In light of the dire situation in Mainland China, some entrepreneurs decided to have their textile machinery shipped to Hong Kong instead and set up factories here. For instance, Nanyang Cotton Mill (南洋紗廠), Hong Kong Spinners (香港紗廠), Kowloon Spinners (九龍紗廠), South Sea Textile Manufacturing Company (南 海 紗 廠) and Grand South Cotton Mill (大 南 紗 廠) set up factories one after the other in Kowloon, laying a strong foundation for the textile industry in Hong Kong. In addition, these manufacturers had much experience in the import and export business. Their knowledge helped Hong Kong make the transition from a trading centre to an industrial one.

To further develop the industrial sector, infrastructure, such as roads, ports, piers and public facilities, was enhanced. After the war, newly-built factories were concentrated in Tai Kok Tsui, To Kwa Wan and Hung Hom. Later, some factories were built in Cheung Sha Wan and San Po Kong. The industrial sector in Tai Kok Tsui had been developed by the 1930s and there was not much room left for growth in the late 1940s. However, a large piece of reclaimed land in Cheung Sha Wan attracted many businessmen to set up factories in the areas along Cheung Sha Wan Road, Lai Chi Kok Road and Castle Peak Road. Industrial areas such as Sham Shui Po, Shek Kip Mei and Cheung Sha Wan grew rapidly, with the textile industry being particularly successful.

Kowloon City in 1950. Kowloon City Bus Terminus is in the centre of the photo, offering routes to Sai Kung and Clear Water Bay. Route 1 carried passengers to Tsim Sha Tsui Ferry Pier.

The junction of Sham Shui Po's Un Chau Street and Tai Po Road. Vehicles needed to use this road to access the New Territories.

Around 1955, 2 brand new Daimler A double-deck buses at Tsim Sha Tsui Ferry Pier terminus. Made in the UK, the bus model was equipped with 56 seats and allowed another 17 passengers to stand. The seats and floors were made of wood. The Daimler A was retired in 1983.

The section of Nathan Road near Yau Ma Tei's Pitt Street around 1955. On the right is a Route 9 bus.

An aerial view of Tsim Sha Tsui Ferry Pier and Kowloon Wharf. Photo taken in 1962.

A bus on Route 16A passing through Shanghai Street near the junction of Nanking Street around 1960. The route ran between Jordan Road Ferry Bus Terminus and Tsuen Wan West.

A bus on Route 12 passing through Reclamation Street around 1965.

In 1949, the population density in urban areas was extremely high, about 50,000 people per square kilometre – a figure which changed little right into the 1970s. In 1949, people lived in three- to four-storey buildings, while 20 or so years later, many residential buildings already had 10 or more storeys. In short, Hong Kong faced a tremendous population problem after the war – a population which stood at around 1.55 million in 1946 rose to 2.02 million in 1951. This figure became 2.61 million in 1956 and 3.17 million in 1961.

The population of Hong Kong doubled in just 15 years, an increase greater than any city can easily sustain. A large number of these people lived in Kowloon, posing a huge challenge to public services. Thus, half of the 1961 population, or 1.6 million, lived in Kowloon (including New Kowloon). The number of residents living on Hong Kong Island was 1.03 million. The population of Kowloon surged again to 2.08 million in 1966 while that of Hong Kong Island dropped to 940,000. In 1971, the population of Kowloon reached 2.32 million while that of Hong Kong Island further dropped to less than 830,000.

Problems caused by dramatic population growth

Most of the workforce resided in old districts such as Yau Ma Tei, Mong Kok, Tai Kok Tsui and Sham Shui Po. After a fire broke out in the Shek Kip Mei squatter area in 1953, the Resettlement Department and Hong Kong Housing Authority built many public housing estates and resettlement blocks. They were located in Shek Kip Mei, Tai Hang Tung, Lei Cheng Uk, So Uk, Wang Tau Hom, etc. Starting from the 1960s, more estates were built in Tseun Wan, Tai Wo Hau, Jordan Valley, Kwun Tong, Tsz Wan Shan, Choi Hung, Ngau Tau Kok, Sau Mau Ping, Yau Tong, Ho Man Tin, Hung Hom, Ma Tau Wai, Pak Tin, Cheung Sha Wan, Kwai Chung, Lam Tin, etc. Many of these were built on a relatively large scale and housed tens of thousands of residents. Large resettlement areas such as Tsz Wan Shan, Sau Mau Ping and Wong Tai Sin housed more than 100,000 people. This number is actually the population of a mid-sized city in many countries. Within just 10 years, farmland, hill slopes and squatter areas were turned into communities with high population densities. The challenge to carry out urban planning and arrange public transport was daunting.

Ngau Chi Wan Bus Terminus in 1963.

Lo Fu Ngam (now Lok Fu) under development in 1962. Lo Fu Ngam Bus Terminus is on the left.

Buses running along Shatin Pass Road in Wong Tai Sin around 1960.

Tsz Wan Shan (North) Bus Terminus in 1968. Only Routes 3B and 3C served local residents.

In addition to building public housing estates, the government amended the Buildings Ordinance in 1956, which waived the height limit imposed on residential buildings in 1936. This amendment would allow the government to utilise more land and therefore provide more housing. Many high rises, such as Man King Building and Man Wai Building by Jordan Road Ferry Pier, were built in subsequent years. There were more than 100,000 residents in only 8 buildings, a number comparable to that of a large public housing estate. Imagine one-third of the residents leaving the estate for work or school with bus services having to accommodate that number - there would have been tremendous pressure on the bus company.

An aerial view of the Tsz Wan Shan area under construction. There were a total of 66 resettlement buildings in that area - the largest number in Hong Kong. Initially there was a shortage of bus services and residents had trouble commuting to other places.

A Route 14 bus in front of the newly-built Choi Hung Estate in 1963.

The most representative bus route at the time was 6D running between Lai Chi Kok and Ngau Tau Kok. The route first commenced operations in 1958. It departed from Lai Chi Kok Amusement Park and carried passengers to both new and old industrial areas, such as Sham Shui Po, Boundary Street, Kowloon City, Ngau Chi Wan and Cheung Sha Wan Factory Estate, where family-owned industries were concentrated. With the construction of new roads and city development, buses on Route 6D were re-routed to go by Cheung Sha Wan Road, Kom Tsun Street and Castle Peak Road. Popular with passengers who worked at cotton mills in Lai Chi Kok and the industrial zone in Cheung Sha Wan, Route 6D witnessed Hong Kong's industrial growth, economic advance and the decline of the industrial sector after manufacturers moved their factories up north.

Choi Hung Road in San Po Kong. Not long after 1963, the area was developed as an industrial zone. The cluster of huts is a temporary housing area.

Small factories in Ngau Tau Kok in 1965. Resettlement blocks were later built in the area (later known as Lower Ngau Tau Kok Estate).

In the early 1960s, the major termini in Kowloon were located at Tsim Sha Tsui Ferry Pier, Lai Chi Kok Amusement Park, Kowloon City Ferry Pier and Jordan Road Ferry Pier. Garment factories flourished in the area of Kowloon City Ferry Pier. Larger ones like Asia Garment Factory employed several hundred workers. Many female workers commuted to and from work on Route 2E. Former bus captain Sin Sing remembers how bus captains who operated the route frowned when they saw the Whampoa Dockyard workers in the Wuhu Street area. This was because hundreds of workers flocked to get on the buses after work. Occasionally, the workers quarrelled and things even turned violent. Furthermore, stains left on the passenger seats were hard to remove.

Route 6 operating between Lai Chi Kok and Tsim Sha Tsui commenced services in the 1940s (originally as Route 2), carrying passengers to Cheung Sha Wan, Mong Kok, Yau Ma Tei and Tsim Sha Tsui. During this period, the average salary had increased slightly, giving residents greater purchasing power. As a result, catering and entertainment industries thrived. Besides taking them to work, Route 6 had to carry passengers to and from the Yau Tsim Mong District to relax. It was definitely the most multi-functional of all KMB routes.

Resettlement blocks under construction in Ngau Tau Kok in 1967. A temporary bus terminus is shown at the bottom of the photo.

Woh Chai Street in Shek Kip Mei in 1972. The 3 yellow stripes on the front of the Route 2E bus means that there is only 1 conductor on board.

Sau Mau Ping (Central) Bus Terminus in 1974.

A single-deck bus on Tung Tau Tsuen Road in 1975, when single-deck buses still operated on many routes in Kowloon.

A unique view of Hong Kong: a double-deck bus passing public housing estates. Photo taken at Ho Man Tin Estate in 1975.

Route 2D departing from Pak Tin in 1975.

Lei Muk Shue Bus Terminus in 1975.

A Route 4 bus arriving at Jordan Road Ferry Bus Terminus around 1960.

Jordan Road in the early 1960s when there was a mix of old and new buildings.

Before the 1970s, living conditions in Hong Kong were far from ideal. People were crammed in small units and hygiene conditions were poor. For example, in resettlement areas (which had a combined population of over 1 million, with the majority residing in Kowloon), one person occupied an average area of 24 square feet. In other words, a standard 120 square foot unit housed 5 people. If there were children in the household, the average area occupied by each person would be even lower. For many people, a home was synonymous with a bed and they subsisted on a meagre salary. In 1966, the starting daily wage for workers was $4-5, while the wage for skilled workers was $9. Many people only made about $100 each month and they could not afford to travel abroad. Subscribing to Rediffusion Television, which was established in 1957, was very expensive. Initially, only English programmes were broadcast, with a Chinese channel being introduced in 1963. Back then, television, still a novelty, was not a popular form of entertainment. In their leisure time, people visited the countryside, watched movies or went swimming. Take a Kwun Tong resident as an example. If he liked to go swimming, he would first go to Choi Hung on Route 14A and then go to Clear Water Bay on Route 21. The fare for the two bus rides came to 50 cents (20 cents + 30 cents). If he wanted to go to Castle Peak, he would first go to Sham Shui Po on Route 2D and then take Route 16 or 16C (which ran only on holidays) to Castle Peak. The total fare was $1 (20 cents + 80 cents). Low bus fares allowed the public to commute to different parts of Hong Kong for weekend activities.

Jordan Road Ferry Pier in 1965. Adjacent to it are the newly-built Man King Building and Man Wah Building. In their heyday in the early 1970s, each of these buildings housed over 10,000 residents.

Birth of satellite towns

To alleviate the problem of overcrowding and create more land for new industries, in 1953 the government started planning the development of Kwun Tong and Tsuen Wan, known as "satellite towns" since they were on the periphery of the urban areas. By building satellite towns and new towns, the government aimed to provide enough housing and job opportunities for Hong Kong people, while alleviating the housing and employment problems faced in old areas. This was also a way of relieving traffic congestion. It was the first time Hong Kong utilised an integrated approach to urban planning. Based on the two principles of "self-sufficiency" and "balanced development", industrial and commercial zones needed to be built in satellite towns in addition to housing areas. Tsuen Wan (including Kwai Chung) and Kwun Tong grew so rapidly that they became the major industrial centres in Hong Kong in just a few years. The development blueprint for Tsuen Wan released in 1959 indicated that the new town was intended to accommodate 1.2 million people – more than one third of Hong Kong's entire population at the time. This was undoubtedly very ambitious.

Kwun Tong, one of the satellite towns, under development in 1962.

Tsuen Wan's Castle Peak Road in 1962. Tai Wo Hau is seen in the background.

Initial stage of the development of Tsuen Wan in 1962.

An aerial view of Tsuen Wan in 1963. Tai Chung Road is now where the canal is in the photo. Fuk Loi Estate is under construction in the background.

But the development did not go as expected. As of 1990, the population of Tsuen Wan was around 730,000, only 60 per cent of the estimated population. Nonetheless, the population density was still very high. The dramatic increase in the number of residents during the early development of Tsuen Wan in the 1960s put a strain on public transport. According to government figures, the population of Tsuen Wan in 1964 had increased by 80 per cent compared to 1961. The surge was due to masses of people moving into the district. To meet the increasing demand, KMB placed an order for 70 buses and requested 10 be delivered each month. In addition to expanding the bus fleet, KMB made new arrangements for its routes and terminus facilities. In October 1963, the bus stop at Dragon Inn, located at 19.5 Miles, Castle Peak Road, was completed and became the terminus for the following routes: Route 19 between Sheung Tsuen and Castle Peak, Route 16A between Jordan Road Ferry Bus Terminus and Tsuen Wan West, and Route 16B between Kwai Chung and Sham Tseng.

KMB later set up a bus terminus at Tsuen Wan Ferry Pier, operating routes to and from Mong Kok Ferry Pier as well as Jordan Road Ferry Bus Terminus. The distance covered by the new routes was twice as long as that covered by the two original ones. Unlike many other satellite towns in other parts of the world, Tsuen Wan and Kwun Tong were solely dependent on road transport since they were not equipped with railways or ferries. Buses were therefore the only mode of transportation for the residents (there were no minibuses until 1969 and working-class residents could not afford to commute by taxi). They therefore travelled to work or school and went shopping by bus.

For KMB, the growth of satellite towns should have translated into the expansion of its services. It was, however, another story in reality. To encourage the people of Hong Kong to move to these new towns for housing and work, the government imposed restrictions on bus services. That way, residents would work in the same area instead of looking for work in other places. The measure created many problems since many residents still needed to commute to other districts for work and school. A large number of people, particularly during peak hours, needed to commute between the satellite towns and the urban areas.

Hip Wo Street in Kwun Tong in 1964 with the Route 13A bus terminus.

By 1966, the number of residents in resettlement areas and low-cost housing estates in Tsuen Wan, including Tai Wo Hau, Kwai Chung and Fuk Lok Estates, was over 100,000, but only 10 routes served them (16, 16A, 16B, 16C, 16D, 26, 27, 32, 33 and 34). Worse still, it was mostly single-deck buses that were employed on these routes. Meanwhile, by the first half of 1967, many resettlement blocks and low-cost housing estates had been built in Kwun Tong and Yau Tong, including Kwun Tong resettlement area and a low-cost housing estate, Wo Lok Estate, and Yau Tong resettlement area. With resettlement blocks also established in Lam Tin and

Kwun Tong Road is bustling in 1974.

Sau Mau Ping, the population of the entire district exceeded 100,000. Yet, there were only 8 routes operating (excluding the ones to and from Ngau Tau Kok): 2B, 2C, 2D, 5B, 11B, 11D, 13A and 14A, and single-deck buses were used on some of these routes. With residents dissatisfied with the inadequate bus services, between the end of 1967 and the beginning of 1968, KMB began the operation of limited stop routes for 13D, 14 and 15, which eased the problem slightly. Additionally, starting from 1968, Route 40 was introduced, running between Tsuen Wan Ferry Pier and Kwun Tong Ferry Pier. In the morning it carried passengers to the industrial areas of San Po Kong and Kwun Tong, and in the evening it took them back to their homes in Tsuen Wan and Sham Shui Po.

In an attempt to keep pace with the swift development of Kwun Tong, KMB built a multi-storey bus depot in 1965 to service the buses operating in neighbouring areas. The depot was well equipped and offered services such as repairs, assembly, parking and washing. However, KMB was not able to put into effect its plan to greatly expand its services until around 10 years later, when the government developed new towns on a large scale.

Kwun Tong Ferry Pier Bus Terminus in the 1980s. Before the Cross-Harbour Tunnel was constructed, bus termini were set up next to many ferry piers for passenger convenience.

Former KMB public relations manager, Mr Wong Lam, pointed out that Kwun Tong was a mess in the 1960s when its development had just started. He was then the Operations Officer of the bus depot in Kwun Tong. Various government departments were involved in public transport matters, so KMB had to exchange views with the District Office, the police (it was still in charge of transport as the Transport Department had not yet been established), Social Welfare Department, Home Affairs Department, etc. Before the establishment of the District Councils, this was how district consultations were carried out.

The old Tsuen Wan Ferry Pier bus terminus in the 1980s.

Coordination of bus services

2 buses being washed at the depot in Lai Chi Kok in the 1960s.

With the increase in the population in Kowloon in the 1950s, passenger numbers continued to grow. In 1957, KMB purchased 100 Seddon Mark 17 buses - the biggest transaction of its kind in Hong Kong. That year, the franchise for KMB's bus services was extended to 1960. At the same time, the population of the New Territories continued to rise. Instead of allowing passengers to get off wherever they liked as in the past, KMB began setting up bus stops at specific locations. In the early 1950s, many people commuted by bus, but there was a shortage of vehicles. So buses were often fully loaded and some passengers were even injured trying to squeeze onto a packed bus. Early models were not equipped with any doors, so to board or alight, passengers needed to use the open platform at the back of the bus. Later, KMB installed sliding metal gates at the back. The Daimler A double-deck buses introduced in 1954 were fitted with front doorways. In addition, the bus operator hired conductors to maintain order as passengers got on and off.

This meant that in those days there were 3 KMB staff members on each bus: the bus driver, the ticketing officer and the conductor. The ticketing officer would carry a bag that contained the day's tickets, some change and a hole-punch. Every day before work, he or she would need to record the ticket type and number. When they finished work, they would have to bring the remaining tickets, ticket slips and fares back to the depot. The fares collected would then be counted. To prevent fraud, the ticketing officer would have to make up any discrepancy between the tickets sold and the money collected from their own salary. The coins collected would be put into a wooden tray with 100 slots and would be counted by specified employees. The method was quite primitive yet efficient. Every evening, the sound of coins clinking against the trays could be heard.

In 1960, the government announced that KMB's franchised bus services would be extended for another 15 years. A year later, KMB was listed on the Hong Kong Stock Exchange along with Jardine Matheson and Gilman Holdings Limited. The capital stock was $31,351,600, with 3,135,160 shares and each share priced at $10. When it was first listed, 78,379 shares were sold at $58 each. That was when Hong Kong experienced its first bull market after the war and people bought stocks in earnest. KMB performed very satisfactorily as a new stock.

A lady waiting for a bus in the 1950s at a location which might have been Kowloon Tong. Bus stop poles did not specify routes but just carried the message 'Buses stop here" in Chinese and English.

According to government reports, 1.02 billion passenger trips on public transport (operated by 5 companies) were recorded in Hong Kong in 1963, of which KMB accounted for 514 million passenger trips (the average daily number of passengers was 1.41 million). This figure was almost 2.7 times more than that recorded for Hongkong Tramways, at 191 million passenger trips. The total number of KMB passenger trips in 1963 was 32 million more than in the previous year and the total journey distance covered was 3.96 million miles, which was 1 million miles more than that covered in the previous year. In 1963, KMB operated 425 double-deck buses and 433 single-deck buses on a total of 62 routes, including 36 in Kowloon and 25 in the New Territories. There was also Route 1, which ran on Lantau Island between Silvermine Bay and Shek Pik.

While the primary reason for the increase in bus passenger trips was population growth, passengers were beginning to show some changes in their way of life and mindset. A report by the Transport Advisory Committee released in 1964 reads: "Facts show that many people who used to get to places on foot now get around by public transport." The mid-1960s marked a new chapter in the development of bus services. Before then, many residents preferred walking to taking the bus in order to save money. There is a saying that goes "Money is as important as one's life. Ten cents is even bigger than Kowloon City." We can see that people considered commuting by bus a luxury. As the fare between Sham Shui Po's Yen Chow Street and Lai Chi Kok Amusement Park was calculated by section, many passengers did not mind walking further to board the bus at the section point just to save 10 cents. Yet, starting from the mid-1960s, as the economy prospered and the public went out more frequently, getting around by bus became a more and more common part of daily life. For a relatively small city of the size of Hong Kong, the number of passengers carried by KMB on a daily basis is probably unparalleled. Back then, there were neither other means of transport available nor sufficient bus services. To make matters worse, passengers were not accustomed to queuing, and living and working conditions were poor. Therefore, it was not uncommon for passengers to quarrel

Passengers rushing to board a bus at Jordan Road Ferry Bus Terminus in around 1965.

with bus employees. Occasionally, these cases had to be resolved in court. There was a conductor in charge of maintaining order on board, and when the bus was full, conductors needed to stand firm to turn passengers away. To alleviate these problems, the Transport Advisory Committee launched a campaign in 1962 to encourage passengers to line up. It also conducted field research on 200 bus stops to see which ones were the most crowded.

Around 1960, a Route 5B bus passing through To Kwa Wan.

A common sight in the 1960s – passengers jostling with each other to board the bus, at a time when services failed to meet demand.

In the 1960s, Hong Kong society was in a rather messy state, but it was brimming with opportunities. For example, hawkers sold lunchboxes at bus termini during the lunch hour. Passengers could pick the dish they liked and the hawkers would leave once they had sold everything. As they did not have much time to eat, many bus drivers rushed back to the terminus, driving past some bus stops where passengers were waiting without stopping. Worse still, some of them did not depart according to the schedule so that they could have more time for lunch. Back then, when telephones were still not common, passengers had nowhere to turn to lodge their complaints. All they could do was curse as they watched the bus go past.

In view of the huge demand, KMB came up with a few solutions. One was to employ more inspectors and regulators, as well as to provide training for its staff. It also rolled out courtesy campaigns and told its bus captains not to skip stops without reason or stop in undesignated areas. KMB also increased the number of buses in its fleet and operated bigger vehicles on busier routes. Thus, in 1963, the AEC Regent V, which was 34 feet long, came into operation. This particular model could carry over 120 passengers and was even bigger than some of the buses used in the UK. After that, more and more double-deck buses were added to KMB's fleet. To protect passengers' safety, KMB began installing automatic doors on buses in 1963. By 1965, 353 buses had been fitted with such doors.

Major bus stops were gradually equipped with rails to help people line up under the oversight of regulators. That was when passengers started to form the habit of lining up. Leung Mei-fan, one of KMB's first female ticketing officers in 1967, remembers that she had to undergo several months of training before selling tickets in the New Territories. She was instructed by experienced ticketing officers on how to stand firm on the moving bus by spreading her feet apart and told to stay on high alert so that nobody would try to take the bus without paying. She remembers a group of mischievous students who tried to do just that. She ended up playing hide-and-seek with them and managed to grab a schoolbag off one of them. Taking out a textbook and finding out where they studied, she was able to inform their teachers of their delinquency.

A news report on the courtesy campaign by KMB in 1963.

Jordan Road Ferry Bus Terminus in the late 1960s, at that time the busiest bus terminus. Many long distance routes to the New Territories departed from here. The facilities were improved after renovations in the mid-1960s.

Tsim Sha Tsui Ferry Pier Bus Terminus in 1970. The AEC Regent V, the bus model with the highest passenger capacity which was used on Routes 5 and 6, is shown on the left.

In the past, bus stops were equipped with few facilities. There was a pole that stated "Buses stop here" and passengers were not protected from the elements. Since the 1950s, major bus termini like the one at Kowloon City Ferry Pier began to be fitted with shelters. By 1964, large bus termini had been established at So Uk, Choi Hung, Wong Tai Sin, Wang Tau Hom, Hung Hom, Tsuen Wan, Yuen Long, etc. More bus stops were set up around the territory as more routes commenced operations.

The small bus depot located in Sham Shui Po was unable to handle the growing demand for bus services, so in 1965 depots in Kwun Tong and at Po Lun Street in Lai Chi Kok came into use. These multi-storey depots were very advanced for their time. To sum up, KMB was developing rapidly in the 1960s. In 1961, the daily number of passenger trips reached 1 million, rising steeply to 1.77 million before the 1967 disturbances in Hong Kong.

A bus on Route 15B passing through Sha Tin Market around 1965.

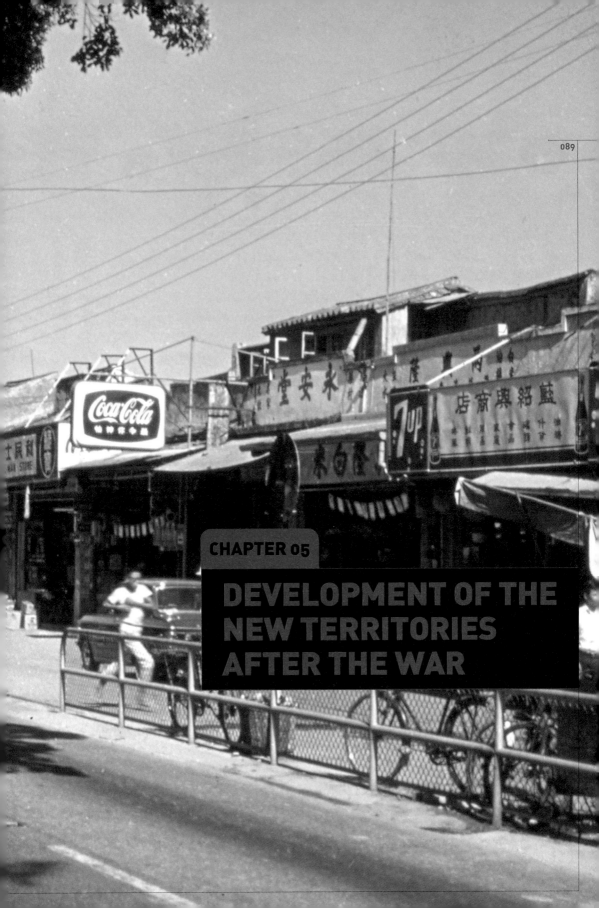

CHAPTER 05

DEVELOPMENT OF THE NEW TERRITORIES AFTER THE WAR

Opening of roads in the New Territories

Before World War II, the New Territories used to be a rural area. Conventional farming slowly declined towards the end of the 1940s and the industrial as well as commercial sectors began to develop. As the transport network was not well developed before the war, commercial activities were mainly concentrated in Yuen Long and Tai Po. After the war, the population soared while living conditions on Hong Kong Island and in Kowloon deteriorated. Many newly arrived immigrants settled in the New Territories since the rent and living costs there were relatively low. This resulted in a dramatic increase in the population in the area, which in turn benefited the growth of its industrial and commercial sectors. Commercial activities expanded into industrial areas, barracks and even schools, and small-scale shops and private organisations invested money in renovating their premises for business purposes. As a result, in just a few years, new and old towns, such as Tsuen Wan, Castle Peak (Tuen Mun), Yuen Long and Sheung Shui, had been given a complete makeover. As a guide to the New Territories published in 1952 puts it, "areas which used to be quite barren are now bustling with energy."

The industrial sector in the New Territories was relatively small before the war and many start-ups were family-owned. Industries on a bigger scale, including brick, lime and porcelain production, depended heavily on labour. After the war, thanks to the population growth and the introduction of factory machinery, a new era was ushered in. Enamel factories, cotton mills and fur fabric factories in Tsuen Wan, beer factories in Sham Tseng, porcelain and brick factories in Castle Peak, and fur factories in Yuen Long, were established or expanded. As the industrial sector in the New Territories thrived, more roads were needed.

Before World War II, the two major roads in the New Territories were Tai Po Road and Castle Peak Road. In addition, Sha Tau Kok Road and Sai Kung Road linked up the northeastern parts of the New Territories. From the late 1940s, the government committed itself to opening more roads in the New Territories and more than a dozen were built in just a few years. The newly-built roads include the following:

A road in the New Territories in the early 1950s. The standard of the roads in the rural areas of the New Territories was generally high and they were able to accommodate quite heavy vehicles.

Lam Tsuen Valley in the early 1950s. On the right is the newly-built Lam Kam Road.

A section of Castle Peak Road near Kwai Chung around 1950. On the left are farmland and villages, which would become an industrial area a decade or so later.

Lam Kam Road: planning started in 1947 and construction began 2 years later. Stretching from Tai Po's Lam Tsuen to Kam Tin, it was completed at the end of 1950. The road is 12 miles long and passes 16 walled villages. There are very few bends. The road slopes first up and then down. Most parts of the road are covered by cement and some by asphalt, making driving on the road relatively safe.

Fan Kam Road: linking to Lam Kam Road and completed in around 1950, it is 5 miles long and allows people to travel between Fanling and Kam Tin. When it first opened, only military vehicles were allowed to use it.

Route Twisk: constructed by prisoners-of-war and villagers under the coercion of the Japanese army during the Japanese Occupation, it provided access to the military radar station at the top of Tai Mo Shan. After the war, the government continued work on the original road and it was completed in 1952. Divided into 15 sections, it is 15 miles long. As it was built on mountainous terrain, its construction was much more taxing than that of Lam Kam Road, requiring large quantities of labour and materials.

After this spate of construction, the northern and southern parts of the New Territories were connected. In addition to the three roads mentioned above, roads linking the following places were built during the same period: Ping Shan and Lau Fau Shan, Ping Shan and Deep Bay, Lau Fau Shan and Deep Bay, Lau Fau Shan and Lung Kwu Tan, Yuen Long and Shap Pat Heung, and Sheung Shui and Lo Wu, as well as Sai Sha Road.

Characteristics of transport in rural areas

Following the development of industrial as well as commercial activities and the opening of new roads, the number of buses operating in the New Territories increased. Back in 1950, only 7 routes operated between Kowloon and the New Territories. Five of them ran from Jordan Road Ferry Bus Terminus to: Man Kam To; Yuen Long; Tsuen Wan; 13 Milestone; and Castle Peak Road. The other two connected: Kowloon City and Clear Water Bay, and Kowloon City and Sai Kung. The 2 routes from Jordan Road Ferry Bus Terminus to 13 Milestone and to Castle Peak Road operated on weekends and holidays only. In 1964, 25 routes were operated between Kowloon and the New Territories (excluding the Lantau Island route) as buses became the main means of transport linking the two regions. Despite this, bus services in the New Territories were not as frequent as those in Kowloon. In a news report published on November 24, 1957, the Sai Kung Rural Committee discussed the enhancement of bus services with KMB. They eventually agreed on changing the location of the bus terminus. However, KMB did not agree to increase the number of vehicles since there were not enough passengers. Back then, 3 buses ran between Sai Kung and Kowloon City Ferry Pier at a frequency of 90 minutes.

Meanwhile, the bus routes that operated in other parts of the New Territories were more frequent than those serving Sai Kung, with Route 16 running between Jordan Road Ferry Bus Terminus and Yuen Long carrying the most passengers. In 1957, 26 buses operated on this route each day. At Chinese New Year, 8 extra buses would be dispatched as Yuen Long organised the biggest market in New Territories West. KMB also set up a depot in the area that ensured the maintenance of its bus fleet there.

The KMB depot in Yuen Long in the 1960s. Besides bus parking, some maintenance work was carried out at the single-storey depot.

The hustle and bustle of Castle Peak Road (Yuen Long section) in the late 1960s.

As there were fewer passengers on rural routes, in 1963 the government approved the adjustment of fares for return journeys on rural routes, introducing section fares after entering urban areas. This meant fares for buses on New Territories-Kowloon routes would be the same as those on urban routes upon entering the city. It was hoped that these buses would attract some of the passengers who originally took the urban routes, maximising the capacity of rural routes and reducing the overcrowding on urban ones. Bus services offered in the New Territories differed from those in urban areas in other ways apart from the number of buses, routes and passenger capacity. These differences serve to illustrate that the residents of the two areas had different ways of life. After the war, Kowloon developed quickly and passengers commuted to work or school by bus. On the other hand, the New Territories remained predominantly rural and many of its residents subsisted on farming and transported their goods by bus. Different fare systems were also in place for these two groups of passengers. In the New Territories, when a passenger carried goods, they would need to buy a ticket for them too. According to the regulations released in 1955, passengers had to pay half fares for goods or luggage weighing 10-50 pounds. If the goods or luggage weighed 50-100 pounds, they had to pay full fare for them. Passengers were not allowed to bring on board goods or luggage weighing more than 100 pounds. Moreover, no fresh fish over 10 pounds was allowed onto the bus and passengers could carry two fishing rods at most.

Tai Po Market in 1958 with a Route 23 bus. This route, which ran between Tai Po Market and Yuen Long, has been changed many times and is now 64K.

A bus on Route 90 on its way to Rennie's Mill (Tiu Keng Leng) via Po Lam Road South in 1987. The bus retired at the end of 1987. The bus route was cancelled in 1996 because Tseung Kwan O started its development and Tiu Keng Leng (then still called Rennie's Mill) residents moved to other areas.

Route 70 running between Sheung Shui and Jordan was the major bus route which Sheung Shui and Fanling residents took to get to the urban areas where they sold their produce. Mr Lai Ping Kwong, a bus driver on Route 70 in the early 1980s, remembers that passengers with baskets of vegetables would wait for the first bus at around 6 am, gathering in groups of 2 or 3. The bus would pass through Fanling and Tai Po, travel to Kowloon via Tai Po Road, and return to Luen Wo Hui in Fanling. Some passengers would carry produce onto the bus and the bus driver would learn from them what good quality produce was on sale at Mong Kok market that day. The bus driver would also be able to tell when a festival was approaching from the goods carried by passengers. When residents carried home-made rice dumplings, he or she would know that the Dragon Boat Festival was near, and when residents carried home-made mooncakes, it was a sign that the Mid-Autumn Festival was approaching. Sometimes, the food that passengers carried revealed their identities. Some elderly women would carry bamboo baskets of cha guo (a tea cake delicacy with fillings such as coconut, mung bean, peanut or yam) and the bus driver would be able to tell they were of Hakka descent. Since Mr Lai was also a Hakka, he would greet them in the Hakka dialect. The passengers would then inform him if the cha guo was sweet or savoury. Mr Lai also recalls that some passengers would bring on board pots of food items made of Chinese Fevervine. Life was much simpler back then, he says.

The Tai Hing Estate Bus Terminus in Tuen Mun in 1979.

CHAPTER 06

THE TEN-YEAR HOUSING PROGRAMME AND DEVELOPMENT OF NEW TOWNS

The impact of the 1967 disturbances

During the period of social unrest, to protect the bus driver from assault, KMB installed a protective wire mesh on the windshield.

In the 1960s, Hong Kong's economy continued to flourish and the total value of exports increased five-fold in 10 years. However, as the economy grew, many latent problems arose and they catalysed the social upheaval that took place in 1966 and 1967. The 1967 disturbances, needless to say, had a huge impact on Hong Kong and hindered KMB's bus services significantly. Bus drivers who did not go on strike became the targets of assaults. As a result, many employees quit their job and some buses were also destroyed or damaged. KMB was only able to maintain limited services, including 6 routes in Kowloon and 5 routes in the New Territories. To maintain public transport services, the police escorted KMB employees to buses and also carried out patrols more frequently along major routes.

During the 1967 disturbances, a bus was set on fire on Choi Hung Road. Photo taken on May 13, 1967.

Sometimes, they escorted the bus for a few minutes in an attempt to pacify both the bus driver and passengers. Because of the disturbances, KMB lost many of its employees and passengers, and the situation took several years to return to normal. Many bus services were suspended because of the riots and 9-seater minibuses began operating in urban areas. They were licensed in 1969, ushering in the era of minibuses as we know it today, serving as an auxiliary means of transport. The number of seats rose from 9 to 14. The seating capacity was further increased to 16 in 1988 as minibus services became a keen competitor of franchised bus services.

After the disturbances, Governor Sir David Trench recognised that poor living conditions were one of the main driving forces behind the unrest. However, it wasn't until Sir Murray MacLehose took office as Governor in 1971 that significant changes were made. The Governor understood Hong Kong residents' dissatisfaction with their living conditions. In October 1972, he announced the Ten-Year Housing Programme, which aimed to provide public housing for 1.8 million people by 1983. The government estimated that they would need to introduce 72 estates by building new ones and renovating old ones. It was hoped that within 10 years, the people of Hong Kong would no longer be crammed in tiny units and that they would be able to enjoy more public facilities. Later developments showed that the government had been too optimistic in its planning.

Bus services were severely disrupted during the riots. To meet the public demand for transport services, the government allowed minibuses and lorries to operate in urban areas. The photo shows minibuses parked in Kwun Tong during the riots.

Alleviation of overpopulation in urban areas

Central Kwai Chung in 1969. In the foreground are some village houses and at the back is Shek Yam Estate.

An Albion CH13AXL bus passing through a construction site at Cheung Shan Estate in 1976. Cheung Shan was one of the public housing estates built during the new town development of Tsuen Wan.

Much land was required for the Ten-Year Housing Programme, but space in the urban areas was limited and expensive. Besides building new estates and redeveloping a small number of old ones in urban areas, the government decided to develop new towns in the New Territories. In fact, as early as the 1960s, it planned to develop Sha Tin and Castle Peak (later renamed Tuen Mun) as new towns. However, the property market was depressed and the plan was put on hold. Later, the Land and Development Advisory Committee reworked the original plan and selected Tsuen Wan, Sha Tin and Tuen Mun as three trial locations.

When the trial commenced, the scale of the infrastructure in Tsuen Wan was already quite considerable. Areas including Kwai Chung and Tsing Yi were developed in addition to Tsuen Wan. The main task was to build town halls, sports grounds, leisure and recreational facilities, and schools and libraries to compensate for the lack of such things. Meanwhile, public housing estates were constructed on the periphery of Tsuen Wan, particularly in the area of Shing Mun Valley stretching from Tsing Yi to Tsuen Wan North.

Cheung Ching Estate Bus Terminus in 1979, which served the first public housing estate in Tsing Yi. At the front of the bus are two squares. The diagram inside the squares shows that there is a fare collection box on the bus.

Lek Yuen Estate Bus Terminus in Sha Tin in 1975, when residents moved into the estate, the first of its kind in Sha Tin New Town.

Sha Tin was originally the valley on either side of Tide Cove. In 1973, the government began a large-scale reclamation project there. The sea was reduced to a channel, which is today's Shing Mun River. Several major estates and the town centre were established on the reclaimed land and Fo Tan was developed as an industrial area. Since it was not too far away from Kowloon and there were road and rail links, Sha Tin soon attracted the investment of property developers. Private housing estates and big shopping malls were built and Sha Tin has since become a multi-faceted town.

An aerial view of Sha Tin New Town in 1977.

Tai Hing Estate under construction in 1976. It was the first public housing estate to be built in Tuen Mun after it was selected for development as a new town.

The development of Tuen Mun lagged behind that of Sha Tin since Tuen Mun was further away from Kowloon, and Hong Kong's economic structure was changing. Many factories were moving north to Mainland China, and so fewer job opportunities were available. Moreover, the investment in Tuen Mun was limited. Many residents had to travel long distances to go to work each day. The successful development of Tuen Mun thus mainly depended on its transport network. The case of Tuen Mun shows that new towns cannot be cut off from urban areas entirely, however self-sufficient they might be. Improving the transport network with other areas became an important factor for the design and planning of subsequent new towns.

Mr Woo Kin Keung, General Manager of Tuen Mun Depot, has worked for KMB for almost 40 years. He recalls that when he first joined the company in 1974, there were only a few dozen buses at Yuen Long Depot and only 2 routes to Kowloon were operated. One was Route 16 to Jordan Road Ferry Bus Terminus via Castle Peak Road. The other was Route 26 to Tai Kok Tsui via Sek Kong Camp*. Each ride would take 2 to 3 hours. At that time, Tuen Mun was still known as Castle Peak. Later, Tuen Mun Road opened and the commuting time was shortened. People were therefore more willing to move to Tuen Mun.

*Routes 16 and 26 have changed to 50 and 51 respectively.

A bus on Route 50 passing through Castle Peak Road in 1977. The journey time of the route was once the longest in the network and it covered the greatest distance from Jordan Road Ferry Bus Terminus to Yuen Long East.

Tuen Mun Road (near Tai Lam) under construction in 1977.

The early development of Tuen Mun New Town in 1978. In the background are newly-built industrial buildings.

Former KMB Chief Inspector Mr Leung Yat Fan worked for KMB for 42 years. Formerly stationed at Tuen Mun Pier Bus Terminus, he remembers that the bus stops near Wu Boon House and Butterfly Estate were packed with 300 to 400 passengers waiting for the buses on Routes 59X and 59M every morning. To alleviate the problem, KMB increased service frequencies and also included intermediate stops. In the late 1980s, as the population of Tuen Mun continued to rise, 12-metre-long double-deck buses operated from Tuen Mun Ferry Pier during the morning peak.

KMB Chief Inspector Mr Lam Pak Kay joined KMB in 1982 and witnessed the growth of Tuen Mun. He said that in the early 1980s, the facilities at Tuen Mun Depot were so limited that it was not even equipped with a fuel tank. Buses that ran on Tuen Mun routes had to fill up at Yuen Long Depot before their next shift. Service and maintenance work also had to be undertaken at Yuen Long Depot. When the KMB Overhaul Centre opened in Tuen Mun in 1983, daily maintenance work could be carried out there for buses on Tuen Mun routes.

An aerial view of Tuen Mun New Town in 1979, with construction in full swing.

Feeder bus terminus outside Tai Po Market Station in 1985.

Villagers getting on a Route 75 bus in 1978. Over the years, this route has been widely used by villagers from Ting Kok and Tai Mei Tuk.

Following Tsuen Wan, Sha Tin and Tuen Mun, new towns such as Tai Po, Fanling, Sheung Shui, Yuen Long, Ma On Shan, Tseung Kwan O, Tin Shui Wai and Tung Chung were developed. New towns undoubtedly eased the problem of overpopulation in urban areas, but they did not achieve their goals of self-sufficiency and balanced development, as they had to rely on urban areas. New towns developed at a later stage tended to be even more remote, so at the crux of their planning was the transport network. Ten years after the development of the new towns began, Hong Kong showed an interesting growth phenomenon – many small or mid-sized towns began developing outside the usual urban areas. These towns were connected to urban areas by rail and bus (Appendix 2).

In 1990, the total population of the new towns reached 2.2 million, about one-third of the whole population of Hong Kong. The populations of Tsuen Wan, Sha Tin and Tuen Mun were 730,000, 500,000 and 360,000 respectively. The development of new towns effectively helped resolve the problem of insufficient land at a relatively low cost, which maximised economic efficiency. At the same time, it also improved the living conditions for millions of residents.

Sheung Shui New Town under development in 1985.

San Tsoi Street in Sheung Shui in 1981. At the time, buses still served to connect villages in rural areas.

Sheung Shui Bus Terminus in 1984. Providing rail interchange services was one of the top priorities of KMB. We can see from the photo that KMB adopted a new logo which was designed in 1983. The logo has two colours: cream and red. The design resembles a road system (roads, bridges and auxiliary roads), signifying that the fleet travels in all directions. If viewed from another angle, the logo resembles the letter "K" of KMB and the Chinese character for the number "9" (the first character of KMB's Chinese name).

Yuen Long New Town at the initial stages of development in 1983.

The bay being reclaimed in Tseung Kwan O New Town in the early 1980s.

Trial operations of KMB in Ma On Shan New Town.

Development of the bus network

A golden opportunity for growth arose for KMB when the Cross-Harbour Tunnel opened in 1972. There were initially 3 routes: 101, 102 and 103, jointly operated by KMB and China Motor Bus Company. In the following year, Route 104 commenced operations. The four cross-harbour routes were more expensive than Kowloon routes, but they were very popular since passengers no longer had to interchange from bus to ferry and then back to bus. In 1977, the number of passengers rose by 25 per cent when there were 11 routes operating.

In 1988, 8 KMB routes between Yuen Long and Tuen Mun were cancelled after the Light Rail Transit (LRT) commenced operations. In spite of the cancellation, between 1985 and 1991, the number of routes still increased by a yearly average of 7.3 per cent, with many of the new routes running between new towns. Another group of figures also reflects the correlation between road transport and the development of new towns: while a total of 54 routes were operating in the New Territories in 1975, in 1996*, this number had jumped to 223. In the same period, only 21 routes were added in Kowloon (cross-harbour routes excluded).

* Statistics from 1996 are used here and in the following chapters, as a number of Kowloon and the New Territories routes were run by other franchised bus operators from that year.

Po Lam Bus Terminus in 1987. Po Lam Estate was still under construction at the time when the photo was taken. However, the schools nearby had already opened and KMB had to operate bus services so that students could go to school by bus.

A cross-harbour bus on Route 104 passing through Des Voeux Road Central in 1976.

A bus on Route 73 passing through a housing estate in Tai Po in 1985. The route aimed to provide services for people who lived far away from the train station. The corrugated roof of the bus stop was a typical design in the 1980s and earlier. In 1991, it was replaced by aluminium.

A bus on Route 91 passing through the nearly-completed Choi Wan Estate in 1978.

In 1996, the average distance covered by KMB buses was 16.4km, 30% more than the distance covered in 1975 (12.4km). Around 40% of the routes were long-distance ones. KMB carried passengers from point to point, sparing them the hassle of using intermediate stops, a measure which helped fuel the development of new towns. For new town residents, buses became their primary means of transport since they could go to urban areas and central points on Hong Kong Island directly (that year, 17 out of 55 cross-harbour routes departed from the New Territories). Nonetheless, the increasing number of routes between the New Territories and urban areas put a strain on road traffic, particularly on Nathan Road, Prince Edward Road, Cheung Sha Wan Road and Kwun Tong Road.

From 1976 to 1996, the population of the New Territories increased by 206%, thanks to the establishment of new towns. At the same time, the population of Kowloon dropped by 16%. In 1996, almost half of the Hong Kong population (46.8%) resided in the New Territories. While in 1976, half of the Hong Kong population (53.8%) lived in Kowloon, by 1996 this figure had dropped to 32%. Massive changes took place over a span of 20 years. In the wake of the population surge in the New Territories, public demand for transport services increased greatly. In 1976, the number of New Territories residents using public transport was around 192,000, but this increased more than 6 times to 1.18 million in 1994. By comparison, the overall increase of passengers in Hong Kong was only 56%. For new towns that were not linked by rail, such as Tuen Mun, Yuen Long and Ma On Shan, buses became the most essential form of transport.

A bus on Route 23 passing through Shun On Estate in 1979. People began moving into this estate and Shun Lee Estate around that time.

A bus on Route 4 on Cheung Sha Wan Road in 1981. The route ran between Cheung Sha Wan and Jordan Road Ferry Pier. It was cancelled 2 years later when the MTR's Tsuen Wan Line came into operation.

Challenges posed by rapid development

Between 1970 and 1996, all the new towns were located in Kowloon and the New Territories, which provided many opportunities for KMB as well as challenges. The fact that the number of bus routes was increasing at such a dramatic rate each year meant that KMB needed an organised and resilient system to deal with every contingency. In addition, it had to face issues prompted by unpredictable situations in Hong Kong as well as abroad.

The Ten-Year Housing Programme in the 1970s pushed up the demand for bus services. However, the UK, where the buses were manufactured, was going through a rough time because of persistent strikes, heavily affecting KMB in the process. In 1970, dockyard workers in the UK went on strike, delaying the shipping of the bodies and chassis of 50 Albion single-deck buses. In 1973, the strikes in the UK disrupted the delivery of 150 new buses and the first 6 chassis could only be shipped in May 1974. At the same time, because of rampant inflation, the manufacturer indicated that they would only sign contracts which did not state the price of the buses since this could only be finalised and confirmed 8 months before they were delivered.

Since the shipping of new buses was often delayed, KMB had to keep operating older ones. In order to maintain service standards, KMB rolled out apprenticeship programmes in the mid-1970s. The company sent apprentices to vocational schools and even sent senior engineers for training in the UK. It also revamped the internal maintenance system and set up a new plant to retread tyres using new technology. In the late 1970s, as overseas manufacturers failed to ship buses on time, KMB set up a depot in Tuen Mun to assemble vehicles and manufacture parts so that it would be less dependent on overseas suppliers.

Retreading of tyres in the 1980s.

A large-scale apprenticeship programme was launched in the 1970s to enhance the internal maintenance system.

KMB Overhaul Centre in Tuen Mun, completed in October 1983, cost $100 million to build. It was the biggest multi-storey depot at the time and was listed in the Guinness Book of World Records.

The first batch of trainee inspectors undergoing training on a bus in 1970. The main role of inspectors was to supervise a team of frontline bus operations staff, handle traffic accidents and provide support to passengers and staff.

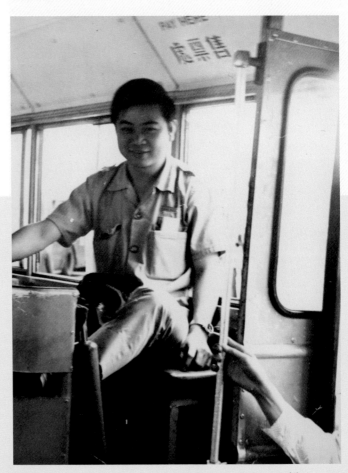

In the early stages of operations, there was no specific ticketing area and 2 to 3 conductors sold tickets to passengers. In 1971, KMB set up a fixed ticketing area on double-deck buses and only 1 conductor was needed.

In the first half of the 1970s, the international political situation was tense and oil prices soared due to the energy crisis. This resulted in persistent global inflation as salaries and the price of commodities rose exponentially. As one of the emerging economies in Asia, Hong Kong was particularly affected. Before the 1970s, the bus service industry was highly labour-intensive. For the morning and evening shifts, 2 bus drivers were required for a double-deck bus. On top of that, there were a total of 6 conductors on both decks, which meant that altogether 8 staff were needed to man each bus on a daily basis.

As operational costs increased, reducing expenditure on salaries became the top priority for KMB. In 1971, therefore, it started to cut the number of conductors from 3 to 1. It also modified the double-deck buses so that there was a ticketing area manned by a single conductor. All passengers had to pass through this area to buy a ticket. In the following year, fare collection boxes were imported from the UK. Conductors were gradually phased out and the position was eliminated by 1982.

A female conductor working on a bus. The seats made of rattan were a hotbed of lice. Synthetic materials have been used since the late 1960s.

In the 1960s, KMB began running training classes for bus drivers. When Sha Tin Depot opened in 1988, it established a school to provide more systematic training.

The key to the operation of bus services is efficiency – the more extensive the coverage area, the more crucial the support of the back office. A bus needs to be fuelled, washed and parked, not to mention having regular service and maintenance. Such tasks need to be carried out close to where the bus operates; otherwise, high costs will be incurred. If a bus were to be fuelled, checked or parked far away from where it operates, fuel consumption would increase and time would be lost, wasting resources and adversely affecting the environment. Moreover, bus parts would be worn out at a faster rate with a further negative impact on costs.

Following the development of Tai Po, Fanling, Sheung Shui, Yuen Long, Ma On Shan, Tseung Kwan O, Tin Shui Wai, Tung Chung, etc., the existing depots-at Kwun Tong and Lai Chi Kok, built in the 1960s, as well as an earlier one at To Kwa Wan, were unable to meet the growing demand for service and maintenance. Therefore, building new depots in areas where buses were concentrated became an important task for KMB.

Sha Tin Depot opened in November 1988. The photo shows the parking area on the top floor.

KMB's Bus Body Construction Depot in Tuen Mun. The assembly task was later outsourced to Zhuhai and the Depot closed in 2008.

The depots serving Tsuen Wan, Kwai Chung and the northwestern districts of the New Territories were the first ones to be developed, including the depot built in Kwai Chung in 1976. Kwai Chung Depot took over the machinery of the warehouse and repairs departments from To Kwa Wan Depot when it was demolished. In 1978, a Bus Body Construction depot where new buses were assembled and fitted was built in Tuen Mun (this depot was closed in 2008). And 1979 saw the opening of Tuen Mun Depot for daily operations and bus service and maintenance. In October 1983, the KMB Overhaul Centre opened in Tuen Mun. Occupying an area of 47,000 sq. metres, the depot can accommodate up to 200 buses. As one of the biggest multi-storey bus depots of its time, the KMB Overhaul Centre was equipped with high-tech facilities, such as brake testers, chassis dynamometers, smoke meters and check-wear testers. November 1988 saw the opening of Sha Tin Depot, consisting of a three-storey bus depot and a six-storey office building, to support Sha Tin, Tai Po and Sheung Shui.

The new Lai Chi Kok Depot opened in 2002.

In the 1990s, Kwun Tong Depot, built in the 1960s, was no longer able to handle the newer and bigger buses. KMB therefore established Kowloon Bay Depot (comprising a three-storey bus depot connected to a four-storey office building) to provide service and maintenance, parking and operational assistance for vehicles running in Kowloon East. Lai Chi Kok Depot experienced the same fate, too. After several decades of operation, it was unable to meet the increasing demand of maintenance work. The fuel depot had already been replaced by private housing estates with high population densities, and incoming and outgoing buses provoked opposition from local residents. As a result, KMB established its new Lai Chi Kok Depot on reclaimed land in the district in May 2002. Bus depots which traditionally had been built on the periphery of urban areas had now, owing to city expansion, to be constructed in more remote locations.

The old Lai Chi Kok Depot completed in 1965. On the left of the photo is Mei Foo Sun Chuen.

Kowloon Bay Depot was completed in 1990 to replace Kwun Tong Depot.

請 合 作

Lok Fu Terminus in 1986. It was one of the earliest bus termini under cover.

CHAPTER 07

NEW CIRCUMSTANCES AND CHALLENGES

Major mode of public transport

After the war, faced with a unique geographical location, the pressure of a growing population and the demands accompanying constant economic growth, the government put the focus of its traffic policies on public transport. As developed areas ran out of land and the room for expanding road capacity was limited, Hong Kong faced difficulties in developing its transport network. To maintain acceptable levels of road capacity, the government enforced a policy that gave public transport priority when it came to road use.

Not only did the government discourage residents from purchasing private cars, but it also curbed the growing number of such vehicles. Consequently, the rate of private car ownership remained rather static between the early 1970s and early 1990s at around 13%. In view of Hong Kong's economic growth, this rate was very low. Up until 1996, 90% of the public commuted by public transport. This averted many of the problems facing developed and partly developed regions where traffic congestion is prevalent because of the large number of private vehicles on the road. Having different means of transport which complement one another is, in fact, the most economical approach.

Allowing modes of transport like the bus to have priority in road usage can alleviate traffic congestion. Buses take up less than 10% of road capacity, but carry one-third of the passenger flow volume. When compared with other vehicles, buses carry the greatest passenger flow volume per unit of road capacity. Moreover, as well as being a less expensive means of transport in the 1970s and 1980s than the train, bus services were more flexible than trains since bus routes could more easily adapt to the ever-changing needs of passengers. This advantage was especially vital in terms of the developing districts. But in areas not covered by railways, buses, while they remained the main transport mode, were subject to certain disadvantages, such as longer journey times caused by traffic jams and occasional service disruptions.

Lower Wong Tai Sin Estate in 1978.

Coordination of buses and trains

Following the economic takeoff in the 1960s and 1970s, Hong Kong began to prosper. The city's GDP per capita reached US$4,100 in 1981, the highest of the Four Asian Tigers. In subsequent years, local productivity increased at a moderate rate and the middle class continued to expand. Meanwhile, government and public demand for better public transport services was much greater than in the years prior to the 1970s.

A feeder bus on Route 76K passing through Kwu Tung in 1984.

According to the Green Paper on transport policies (1974) and the White Paper (1979), the government had already explicitly indicated that the Hong Kong public transport system needed to be geared towards mass transit as early as the 1970s. Conventional mass transit, such as bus and tram services, would be subordinated to the Mass Transit Railway (MTR). Following the opening of the MTR (1979) as well as LRT (1988) and the introduction of railway electrification (1982 to 1983), the railway system became the fastest-growing form of transport and gradually became the core of the public transport network. Because of this "rail-first" policy, restrictions were imposed on bus routes. To avoid direct competition, services could not overlap those provided by trains (buses were not allowed to cover more than 4 train stops). In an effort to raise overall revenue, the KCR (including the LRT) operated their own feeder bus services so that passengers could interchange easily.

In 1986, the government implemented the Public Transport Intermodal Coordination Policy, encouraging residents of the New Territories to commute to urban areas by rail. The policy required

During the early development of Ma On Shan New Town, KMB began operating Route 85K which connected it to Sha Tin Station.

that the final stop for buses should not go beyond Jordan Road for routes from the New Territories or beyond Argyle Street in Mong Kok for routes departing from the housing estates in New Territories East. For routes that departed from the housing estates in New Territories West, the final stop should not go beyond Yen Chow Street in Sham Shui Po. Furthermore, KMB was not allowed to operate routes running between the New Territories and Hong Kong Island. The measures deprived the public of the right to select their preferred form of public transport and caused strong opposition from residents of the New Territories.

The Public Transport Inter-modal Coordination Policy resulted in a drastic drop in passengers for KMB. The government, however, was extremely proactive in pushing the bus operator to coordinate feeder bus services with the railway. In 1982, there were a total of 24 feeder bus routes, including 20 M-routes for the MTR and 4 K-routes for the KCR. Between 1986 and 1996, the number of KMB feeder bus routes (including the KCR and MTR) more than doubled from 41 to 99. They became one of KMB's major services and paid dividends for all parties involved.

However, the overall traffic conditions of Hong Kong were to change soon after the enforcement of the Public Transport Inter-modal Coordination Policy. In 1988, the passenger capacity of the KCR and the MTR reached saturation point and the latter even imposed surcharges during rush hour. That year, the government relaxed the restrictions placed on bus routes travelling between the New Territories and urban areas. In the meantime, the District Councils showed their support for the expansion of bus services, including some of the proposed routes previously vetoed by the government, such as cross-harbour routes from the New Territories. Many of the new routes were express routes set up to attract passengers who previously commuted to the urban areas by train.

The road network outside the Cross-Harbour Tunnel in Hung Hom in 1973. When the Cross-Harbour Tunnel opened in 1972, KMB and China Motor Bus jointly operated three cross-harbour Routes - Routes 101, 102 and 103. They were extremely popular with the public with over 45,000 trips per day.

In 1988, after the government relaxed the Public Transport Intermodal Coordination Policy, KMB instantly set up Route 81C, which was the first franchised route between New Territories East and Tsim Sha Tsui.

In 1996, there were a total of 25 express routes running between the New Territories and urban areas, compared to only 15 in 1986. To shorten the journey time, some of the routes even skipped circuitous sections during peak hours so that passengers might get to their destinations more quickly. These limited stop routes increased from 7 in 1986 to 83 in 1996. There were also special services for some routes during the rush hour - they skipped certain stops in order to cater for passengers who did not need to go to the terminus.

At the same time, the number of cross-harbour routes increased significantly. With the completion of the Eastern Harbour Tunnel and the thriving economy, the number of cross-harbour routes rose from 10 in 1975 to 55 in 1996. In 1996, the number of passengers using the MTR, KCR and LRT was 30% of the total number of people utilising public transport. 26% (1.032 billion passenger trips) travelled by KMB. The number had stood at 38% (934 million passenger trips) in 1979 when the MTR first opened. Despite the drop, a quarter of the passengers using public transport still made their journeys using KMB, a clear indication that the bus operator was staying competitive.

To prevent passengers who did not commute by rail from abusing feeder bus services, the KCR and KMB reached an agreement in 1996, the latter imposing charges in accordance with the rules and regulations of franchised bus services.

Entering the 21st century, as the railway network swiftly expanded to new towns, more and more people were able to take the KCR or MTR near their housing estates. As a result, feeder buses on M-routes and K-routes taking passengers to train stations were not as highly patronised as before. At the same time, a large decrease in passengers caused KMB to suffer financial losses. Despite this, the relevant authorities did not immediately respond to KMB's request to reorganise bus routes, which exacerbated the situation.

Besides the railway, KMB faced fierce competition from ferries, taxis, minibuses (including red minibuses on non-scheduled services and green minibuses on scheduled services), as well as bus operators offering non-franchised bus services and new ones offering franchised bus services. Also, starting from 1982, the government began approving the operation of residential bus services in locations without sufficient minibus or bus coverage. Residents' buses offered point-to-point services, were generally air-conditioned and guaranteed passengers a seat, and thus presented stiff competition to other operators. In addition, the operating hours suited the needs of passengers. Combined together, these factors had a huge impact on franchised bus services. From 1990 to 1996, the number of routes operated by residents' buses jumped from 25 to 136.

Tsim Sha Tsui Star Ferry Bus Terminal in 2003. In the early 1970s, the passenger flow volume of Route 6 was huge and so KMB set up Route 6A in 1974. When the Tsuen Wan Line of the MTR opened, the number of passengers on both routes dropped. In order to distribute resources more evenly and reduce road traffic, the merger of the two routes was proposed and finally took place in 2011.

Improvement of bus models and compartment facilities

Faced with various kinds of competition, KMB responded with different strategies. For instance, it set up new routes in the New Territories and reinforced existing ones. It introduced state-of-the-art air-conditioned buses and super-low floor buses, replaced worn-out vehicles and increased weekend routes as well as express routes. It also arranged special routes during the rush hour, airport buses and all-night services. Overall, the 1990s marked an important chapter for KMB. After a series of improvements, many residents found commuting by bus convenient and also comfortable.

A series of changes had taken place in the 1970s. The average wage had increased and the public expected more from transport services. While in the 1960s, they were content as long as they were able to squeeze onto a bus, they were now demanding comfortable bus rides. Minibuses became one of KMB's competitors after the 1967 disturbances and KMB began operating deluxe single-deck buses in 1975, boasting comfortable seating so that passengers who normally took the taxi could switch to buses. Despite the higher fares, such deluxe buses were very popular with passengers.

With the Kwun Tong Line of the MTR opening in 1979, passengers began demanding air-conditioning in other forms of public transport. In just 3 months, the number of passengers of deluxe buses dropped by 30%, dropping by a further 40% when the Tsuen Wan Line of the MTR came into operation in May 1982. Although the development of new towns soon compensated for the threat posed by the railways, KMB did not stay complacent and worked hard to revamp its bus services to compete with rail. The Mercedes Benz double-deck buses introduced in 1983 represented something of a landmark: the first buses not manufactured in the UK to run in the KMB fleet. As these vehicles were powerful and well-ventilated, passengers embraced them. At the same time, even bigger double-deck buses were introduced, including KMB's double-deck bus with the highest passenger capacity, which carried up to 160 passengers and was fitted with 3 doors.

3 deluxe buses driving towards Tsim Sha Tsui Star Ferry Bus Terminus in 1977. Such buses were not air-conditioned in those days.

In August 1983, Mercedes Benz O305 double-deck buses were introduced and operated on trial, being well received by passengers. They were equipped with a new ventilation method and performed exceptionally on uphill climbs.

KMB's "Airbus" service operated air-conditioned single-deck bus services to and from the airport in the 1990s.

Another strategy employed by KMB was to operate air-conditioned buses. In 1985, Airbus (not to be confused with the aircraft manufacturer) was established to operate airport routes using air-conditioned single-deck buses. In September 1987, small air-conditioned single-deck buses were introduced and they were embraced by passengers. In 1988, KMB successfully introduced Hong Kong's first air-conditioned double-deck bus – the Volvo Olympian. Located in Europe, the manufacturer did not have experience in the production of air-conditioned double-deck vehicles, and so KMB's engineering team were involved in the development stages. Introduced in 2000, the advanced model is equipped with electrostatic filters, which provide more effective filtration of very fine particles, capable of filtering out 80% of fine dust. The buses were also equipped with a thermostat system to adjust the temperature, humidity and air flow, as air-conditioning became one of the prerequisites for new buses. The last batch of non air-conditioned buses retired in 2012.

Another breakthrough for KMB was the introduction of super-low floor buses. One of the policies put forth in 1994 by Governor Chris Patten was to advocate the inclusion of the disabled in society. After getting in touch with many disability groups and organising a number of seminars, he made the suggestion to KMB that many disabled people would like to commute by bus. Mr John Chan Cho Chak, the newly-appointed Managing Director of KMB at the time, on a visit to bus manufacturers in Europe, saw a newly-built super-low floor single-decker in the UK and introduced one such model to Hong Kong in 1996. Later, he asked the manufacturer to produce a super-low floor double-deck bus, the first of its kind in the world, which was introduced in Hong Kong in 1997. There was only one step onto super-low floor buses, which were also equipped with a kneeling device, wheel-chair ramps and a design that improved accessibility for the public, particularly the disabled and the elderly.

In the late 1990s, the design of bus compartment facilities improved significantly, with 2+2 seating adopted on the upper deck. In addition, highly visible handrails were installed, equipped with "Stop" buttons, so that passengers in different parts of the bus could easily press them to alight. Some seats were fitted with seat belts, route maps were provided in the compartment, and a trilingual public announcement system was put in use. The Octopus payment system was gradually introduced and passengers could pay the fares with a swipe of the Octopus card instead of by cash. In the early 21st century, multi-media broadcasting was installed and straight staircases were used to provide passengers with easier access to both decks.

KMB introduced the world's first super-low floor double-deck bus in 1997; its specifications have been used as guidelines for future purchases.

Customer services and route design

To consolidate its customer base, KMB set up a customer service hotline (at peak periods, the hotline receives up to 500,000 enquiries per month) and printed KMB route maps in 1983. In 1992, it set up its first customer service centre at Sha Tin New Town Plaza to handle passengers' comments and suggestions. The public could also purchase KMB merchandise at the customer service centre. The KMB website was launched in 1995, making KMB the first public service organisation in Hong Kong to have its own website. In the early 21st century, the point-to-point route search function was introduced and photographs of bus stops were uploaded onto the website. With KMB's extensive network coverage, all these measures are able to help passengers choose the right services.

To compete with the concourses of railway stations, KMB began revamping the facilities of waiting areas in order to create a better environment and provide passengers with more information. For instance, it built bus stop shelters made of aluminium in 1991 and in terms of information, started listing route details as well as fares. In 1995, display panels with route information and the departure time of the next bus were installed at major termini so that passengers could plan ahead. The Integrated Bus Service Information Display System has also been introduced at major bus termini, providing the most updated route information, including departure time, destination and major traffic incidents. Since 2000, KMB has replaced the roofs of many bus shelters with a material pervious to light but resistant to ultra-violet radiation, noise and heat. In 2009, KMB installed luminous crystal bus-stop poles which allow passengers to check route information at night.

Railways with fixed routes and stations are inherently not as flexible as buses. KMB leveraged this advantage by introducing routes for specific groups of passengers. In 1982, it introduced the first X (Express) routes to urban areas and in 1991, as the railways became more and more crowded, 7 cross-harbour routes using air-conditioned buses in the 300 series were set up, offering an alternative for passengers in the morning. Additionally, special routes, including morning special routes, peak hour special services, festival special routes and green routes, have been added to provide tailor-made bus services for the public. To further enhance its network, KMB introduced the Octopus Bus-Bus Interchange Discount Scheme in 1999, carrying out trial runs on Routes 87A and 88K. The scheme aimed to expand KMB's bus service coverage area and boost its network. The scheme now comprises around 80 interchange packages, covering 60% of KMB's routes.

In the 1990s, an important chapter in the history of the development of bus services was written when China Motor Bus, which ran franchised bus services on Hong Kong Island, pulled out of the market and was replaced by new operators Citybus and New World First Bus. Deputy Chairman of KMB Dr John Chan recalls that the companies posed a threat to KMB with Citybus purchasing many new buses and New World First Bus introducing a brand new fleet. As the public perception of KMB weakened, the company had to consider ways of strengthening its bus services to be more attuned to passenger needs.

A luminous crystal bus-stop pole lit up in the evening.

In pursuit of sustainable development

Maintenance of KMB buses is done in accordance with stringent guidelines. KMB is committed to providing safe and comfortable rides for its passengers.

Just as the operation of bus services faces various challenges at different times, so must the
strategies implemented to handle them vary. At the same time, the basic principles remain the
same: to enhance productivity and better utilise resources with the aim of achieving sustainable
development. In the 1990s, the concepts of environmental protection and quality management
became increasingly important as the ethos of sustainability took hold. KMB responded by taking
these two factors into consideration in its strategic planning.

As far as environmental protection was concerned, KMB introduced in 1992 the environment-friendly
Euro I bus engine, which met the emission standards laid down by the EU; fast forward to 2009 and
it was introducing the Euro V bus engine. In the 1990s, KMB also started a programme of installing
emission reduction devices on older buses, and, at is depots, treating the wastewater from the bus-
washing process so that it could be recycled and re-used. As for fuel, from 2001, all KMB buses used
ultra-low sulphur diesel, and then in 2007 Euro V diesel, the sulphur content of which is only 0.001%,
was adopted fleetwise. All buses were also equipped with the 'Posilock' fuelling system as used on
aeroplanes, which enables fast refuelling without leakage. The company adopted a number of other
green initiatives and organised educational tours at its depots.

In terms of management, KMB became the first public bus company in Hong Kong to implement ISO quality systems, being accredited progressively since 1995 with ISO9001, ISO14001 and OHSAS18001 certification. Since 2000, KMB has introduced a number of facilities which have improved the efficiency of maintenance, operations and management at depots, thereby enhancing productivity and ensuring a more effective distribution of resources.

In 1997, KMB adopted the 'Posilock' fuelling system as used on aeroplanes.

九巴服務 日日進步

KMB received OHSAS18001 certification in 2012, an acknowledgement of its effective management of bus service-related operational risks.

CHAPTER 08

OUTLOOK FOR THE FUTURE

An imminent need for bus route reorganisation

Tuen Mun Road Bus-Bus Interchange opened in December 2012. Passengers can get to different destinations by changing buses at the Interchange (photos above and in the bottom right corner).

Since obtaining the franchise to operate bus services in 1933, KMB has witnessed many of Hong Kong's historic moments as the city's largest bus company while becoming a major and pioneering player on the global transport scene. While its operational record over the past 80 years has proven KMB to be a vibrant and resilient corporation, as it enters its ninth decade of service, KMB faces numerous challenges posed by the ever-changing environment, both locally and internationally.

With the government's promotion of public transport policies that prioritise the railways, the train network has continued its inexorable expansion. On August 18, 2002, the Tseung Kwan O Line commenced operations and KMB lost 100,000 passengers that day. When the Ma On Shan Line opened in 2004, the number of bus passengers dropped once again. Over the past 10 years, 5 railway lines have been established. At its pinnacle in 2002, KMB recorded 3.1 million passenger trips per day, but this has now fallen to 2.6 million. 70% of the 400 bus routes it operates are loss-making and 55% are in desperate need of reorganisation. In the next 5 years, the Sha Tin- Central Line, the South Island Line and the West Island Line will all come into service. If route reorganisation meets significant political resistance, the public will need to subsidise certain routes with continued low patronage and in the long run KMB's operations will suffer (Appendix 3).

Bus route reorganisation aims to speed up and simplify services by enhancing short-distance interchange routes, reducing overlapping routes, merging routes with low patronage, simplifying bus routes and increasing service frequencies. All these measures are geared at enabling passengers to interchange more conveniently. At the same time, long-distance routes would be modified to run on highways as much as possible, making fewer stops and providing more point-to-point services. In this way, passengers would be able to reach their destination in the urban areas more quickly.

Striving for zero emissions

Another challenge facing KMB arises from the general public's growing awareness of environmental protection. In recent years, KMB has been exploring the feasibility of new energy sources in an attempt to reduce carbon dioxide as well as exhaust emissions. In 2010, KMB introduced Hong Kong's first supercapacitor bus, the gBus, for a 6-month trial. An electric bus powered by supercapacitor technology, the gBus is a truly green bus as it produces zero roadside emissions. When fully charged, the gBus can run continuously for 5km and is suited to run on Hong Kong's busy roads, operating smoothly in severe weather conditions such as heat, humidity and thunderstorms. While the supercapacitor and its rapid recharging system proved satisfactory for KMB, in 2012, a newer model of supercapacitor bus, the gBus², was introduced. When fully charged, it is able to run continuously for 8 to 10km, double the distance covered by its predecessor and equivalent to a journey from Tsim Sha Tsui to Kwai Fong. KMB and the manufacturer are currently exploring the possibility of a double-deck supercapacitor bus with zero emissions. In addition to supercapacitor buses, KMB is testing battery-powered electric buses and hybrid diesel-electric vehicles, becoming an industry pioneer in its advocacy of environmental protection.

In 2010, KMB introduced Hong Kong's first supercapacitor bus, gBus, for a 6-month trial.

In 2009, KMB introduced Asia's first double-deck bus with a Euro V engine.

Meanwhile, since the core of the KMB fleet is the double-deck diesel bus, the company continues to pay close attention to the development of green models, introducing, in 2009, the first double-deck bus with a Euro V engine at a time when the law only required newly registered diesel vehicles to meet the Euro IV emission standards laid down by the EU. KMB continues to co-operate with its bus manufacturers in different areas, such as the design and improvement of the air-conditioning system, which will provide more comfortable journeys for passengers while reducing carbon dioxide emissions, and chassis modification for the future deployment of the Euro VI engine.

Entering the smartphone era

As smartphones became more popular, KMB was Hong Kong's first franchised bus operator to launch a mobile app in 2011, allowing passengers to check route information and the most updated services using their phones. A year later, KMB launched a new app with improved functionality, providing information on the latest road traffic conditions. As of today, over 1.2 million users have downloaded the KMB app, making it one of the most popular mobile apps in Hong Kong.

In 2012, KMB introduced the pioneering Estimated Time of Arrival System (ETA System) at the Tuen Mun Road Bus-Bus Interchange. With the help of global positioning technology, the system calculates the arrival time of buses travelling via the interchange and displays the relevant information. KMB was the first bus operator to introduce this technology in Hong Kong. In the future, it is hoped that the ETA System will be able to complement the mobile app so that passengers can find out the arrival time of the next bus on their smartphones.

In 2011, KMB was Hong Kong's first franchised bus operator to launch a mobile app, which is popular with passengers, as it allows them to check route information on their smartphones.

In 2012, KMB introduced the pioneering ETA System at Tuen Mun Road Bus-Bus Interchange, notifying passengers of the arrival time of the next bus.

In 2013, KMB, Hong Kong's longest-running bus company, organised a series of events to commemorate its 80th anniversary. At a celebratory cocktail reception, KMB's Chairman, Dr Norman Leung, said that the company has been a pioneer in the bus industry, and that its passengers always come first (Appendix 4). KMB offers about 2.6 million passenger trips per day with its fleet of approximately 3,800 buses. It runs a total of 392 routes and employs around 12,000 people. It is without a shadow of a doubt a crucial part of Hong Kong's transport network (Appendices 5 to 7).

KMB celebrating its 80th anniversary in 2013. From front left: KMB Director Mr Gordon Siu, KMB Finance & Administration Director Mr William Ho Sai Kei, KMB Corporate Affairs Director Ms Vivien Chan, KMB Commercial Director Mr James Louey, KMB Director Mr William Louey, KMB Director Mr Lui Chung Yuen, KMB Director Mr Eric Li Ka Cheung, Chairman of Transport Advisory Committee Mr Larry Kwok Lam Kwong, Chairman of the Transport Panel of the Legislative Council the Hon. Chan Kam Lam, KMB Managing Director Mr Edmond Ho, KMB Chairman Dr Norman Leung, Chief Secretary for Administration Mrs Carrie Lam Cheng Yuet-ngor, Convenor of the Executive Council the Hon. Lam Woon-kwong, Secretary for Transport and Housing Professor Anthony Cheung Bing Leung, KMB Deputy Managing Director Mr Evan Auyang, Permanent Secretary for Transport and Housing (Transport) Mr Joseph Lai, KMB Director Ms Winnie Ng, Commissioner for Transport Mrs Ingrid Yeung, KMB Operations Director Mr Kenrick Fok, Member of Legislative Council the Hon. Frankie Yick and Deputy Commissioner for Transport/Transport Services & Management Ms Carolina Yip Lai Ching.

Appendix 1

Bus routes, timetable and fares in Kowloon and the New Territories stated in the Government Tender (1932)

Route No.	Details of Route	Hours of Service	Seating Capacity	
			Min.	Max.
1.	Star Ferry & Sham Shui Po, via Salibury Rd., Nathan Rd. & Lai Chi Kok Rd.	From 5.45 a.m. To 1.15 a.m. Every 10 minutes	25	35
2.	Star Ferry & Lai Chi Kok, via Salisbury Rd., Nathan Rd. & Castle Peak Rd.	From 5.45 a.m. To 12.30 a.m. Every 10 minutes	20	35
3.	Star Ferry & Kowloon City, via Salisbury Rd., Chatham Rd., Wuhu St., Taku St., Ma Tau Wei Rd., Tam Kung Rd., Prince Edward Rd. & Sai Kung Rd.	From 5.45 a.m. To 1.15 a.m. Every 10 minutes	20	30
4.	Yaumati Ferry (Jordan Rd.) & Kowloon City via Jordan Rd., Gascoigne Rd., Chatham Rd., Wuhu St., Taku Rd., Ma Tau Wei Rd., Tam Kung Rd., Prince Edward Rd. & Sai Kung Rd.	From 5.30 a.m. To 1.15 a.m. Every 10 minutes	20	30
5.	Star Ferry & Austin Rd., via Salisbury Rd., Nathan Rd., Carnarvon Rd., Kimberley Rd. & Austin Ave.	From 7.30 a.m. To 9.30 p.m. Every 10 minutes	20	20
6.	Star Ferry & Kowloon City via Salisbury Rd., Nathan Rd., Prince Edward Rd. & Sai Kung Rd.	From 5.45 a.m. To 1.15 a.m. Every 10 minutes	20	35
7.	Star Ferry & Kowloon Tong via Salisbury Rd., Nathan Rd., Argyle St., Peace Ave. & Waterloo Rd.	From 6 a.m. To 1.15 a.m. Every 10 minutes	25	30
8.	Yaumati Ferry (Jordan Rd.) & Kowloon Tong via Jordan Rd., Nathan Rd., Prince Edward Rd. & Waterloo Rd.	From 6 a.m. To 1.15 a.m. Every 10 minutes	25	30
9.	Mong Kok Ferry Pier & Un Long Market via Nathan Rd., Castle Peak Rd.	From 5.30 a.m. To 7.30 p.m. Every 1/2 hour	20	20
10.	Star Ferry & Ngau Shi Wan via Canton Rd. to Yaumati Ferry (Jordan Rd.), Jordan Rd., Shanghai St., Prince Edward Rd. & Sai Kung Rd.	From 5.45 a.m. To 12 midnight Every 10 minutes	20	30

Route No.	Details of Route	Hours of Service	Seating Capacity	
			Min.	Max.
11.	Sham Shui Po & To Kwa Wan via Lai Chi Kok Rd., Shanghai St., Yaumati Ferry (Jordan Rd.) Gascoigne Rd., Chatham Rd., Wuhu St., Taku St. & Mau Tau Wei Rd.	From 6 a.m. To 1 a.m. Every 10 minutes	20	25
12.	Star Ferry & Shum Shui Po via Salisbury Rd., Canton Rd., Public Square St., Reclamation St., Shanghai St. & Lai Chi Kok Rd.	From 6.15 a.m. To 12 midnight Every 10 minutes	20	30
13.	Yaumati Ferry (Jordan Rd.) & Kowloon City via Jordan Rd., Nathan Rd., Prince Edward Rd. & Sai Kung Rd. (New route)	From 6 a.m. To 12 midnight Every 10 minutes	25	30
14.	Yaumati Ferry (Jordan Rd.) & Sham Shui Po via Canton Rd., Public Square St., Reclamation St., Shanghai St. & Lai Chi Kok Rd. (New route)	From 6 a.m. To 1 a.m. Every 10 minutes	25	30
15.	Kam Tin & Un Long Market	From 9 a.m. To 5 p.m. (Non Market days) From 7 a.m. To 5 p.m. (Market days) Every 1/2 Hour	15	15
16.	Fan Ling & Tai Po (New route)	From 6 a.m. To 6 p.m. Every 1/2 hour	15	15
17.	Un Long Market & Sheung Shui	From 6.30 a.m. To 5.30 p.m. Every 1/2 hour	15	20
18.	Fan Ling & Sha Tau Kok	From 7.15 a.m. To 6.30 p.m. Every hour	15	20

LIST OF MAXIMUM FARES, KOWLOON & NEW TERRITORIES
Between the undermentioned places, in either direction

	1st Class (Cents)	2nd Class (Cents)
Star Ferry and		
Austin Rd.	10	5
Kowloon Dock Gate	15	10
Mau Tau Kok Rd.	15	10
Kowloon City via Chatham Rd.	20	10
Austin Rd. and		
Kowloon Dock Gate	10	5
Ma Tau Kok Rd.	15	10
Kowloon City	15	10
Kowloon Dock Gate and Kowloon City	15	10
Ma Tau Kok Rd. and Kowloon City	10	5
Yaumati Ferry and		
U.S.R.C.	10	5
Kowloon Dock Gate	15	10
Mau Tau Kok Rd.	15	10
Kowloon City (via Chatham Rd.)	20	10
U.S.R.C. and		
Kowloon Dock Gate	10	5
Ma Tau Kok Rd.	15	10
Kowloon City	15	10
Kowloon Dock Gate and Ma Tau Kok Rd.	10	5
Star Ferry and		
Austin Rd., No.5 Route (1st Class only)	10	-
Pak Hoi St.	10	5
Argyle St.	15	10

	1st Class (Cents)	2nd Class (Cents)
Star Ferry and		
Shum Shui Po	15	10
Waterloo Rd. & Prince Edward Rd.	15	10
Kowloon Tong	20	10
Kowloon City (via Nathan Rd.)	20	10
Ngau Shi Wan	20	10
Yen Chow St.	15	10
Wong Uk Village	20	10
Lai Chi Kok	20	10
Pak Hoi St. and		
Argyle St.	10	5
Shum Shui Po	15	10
Waterloo Rd. & Prince Edward Rd.	15	10
Kowloon Tong	15	10
Kowloon City	15	10
Ngau Shi Wan	20	10
Yen Chow St.	15	10
Wong Uk Village	15	10
Lai Chi Kok	20	10
Argyle Street and		
Shum Shui Po	10	5
Waterloo Rd. & Prince Edward Rd.	10	5
Kowloon Tong	15	10
Kowloon City	15	10
Ngau Shi Wan	15	10

	1st Class (Cents)	2nd Class (Cents)
Argyle St. and		
Yen Chow St.	10	5
Wong Uk Village	15	10
Lai Chi Kok	15	10
Waterloo Rd. and		
Prince Edward Rd. & Kowloon Tong	10	5
Kowloon City	10	5
Ngau Shi Wan	15	10
Kowloon City and		
Ngau Shi Wan	10	5
Yen Chow St. & Wong Uk Village	10	5
Lai Chi Kok	15	10
Wong Uk Village & Lai Chi Kok	10	5
To Kwa Wan and		
U.S.R.C.	10	5
Yaumati Ferry	15	10
Argyle St.	15	10
Sham Shui Po	20	10
U.S.R.C. and		
Yaumati Ferry	10	5
Argyle St.	15	10
Sham Shui Po	15	10
Yaumati Ferry and		
Argyle St.	10	5
Sham Shui Po	15	10
Waterloo Rd. & Prince Edward Rd.	15	10

	1st Class (Cents)	2nd Class (Cents)
Yaumati Ferry and		
Kowloon Tong	15	10
Kowloon City (via Nathan Rd.)	15	10
Argyle St. and		
Waterloo Rd. & Prince Edward Rd.	10	5
Kowloon City	15	10
Mong Kok Ferry Pier and		
Lai Chi Kok	15	10
Tsun Wan.	30	20
Ting Kau	40	25
Tsing Lung Tau	45	30
Tai Lam Chung	55	35
Castle Peak	60	40
Ping Shan	70	50
Un Long	70	50
Lai Chi Kok and		
Tsun Wan	25	15
Ting Kau	30	20
Tsing Lung Tau	45	30
Tai Lam Chung	55	35
Castle Peak	60	40
Ping Shan	70	45
Un Long	70	45
Tsun Wan and		
Ting Kau	10	5
Tsing Lung Tau	15	10
Tai Lam Chung	25	15

	1st Class (Cents)	2nd Class (Cents)
Tsun Wan and		
Castle Peak	30	20
Ping Shan	45	30
Un Long	45	30
Ting Kau and		
Tsing Lung Tau	15	10
Tai Lam Chung	25	15
Castle Peak	30	20
Ping Shan	45	30
Un Long	45	30
Tsing Lung Tau and		
Tai Lam Chung	10	5
Castle Peak	15	10
Ping Shan	30	20
Un Long	40	25
Tai Lam Chung and		
Castle Peak	10	5
Ping Shan	25	15
Un Long	30	20
Castle Peak and		
Ping Shan	15	10
Un Long	25	15
Ping Shan and Un Long	15	10
Sheung Shui and		
Chung Pak Long	5	-
Kam Tin or Siu Yuen	10	-
Chow Tau	15	-
Lok Ma Chau or Sun Tin	20	-

	1st Class (Cents)	2nd Class (Cents)
Sheung Shui and		
Mai Po	25	-
Chuk Yuen, Sun Wai or Fung Kat	30	-
Au Tau	35	-
Un Long	40	-
Chung Pak Long and		
Kam Tin or Siu Yuen	5	-
Chow Tau	10	-
Lok Ma Chow or Sun Tin	15	-
Mai Po	20	-
Chuk Yuen, Sun Wai or Fung Kat	25	-
Au Tau	30	-
Un Long	35	-
Kam Tin or Siu Yuen and		
Chow Tau	5	-
Lok Ma Chau or Sun Tin	10	-
Mai Po	15	-
Chuk Yuen, Sun Wai or Fung kat	20	-
Au Tau	25	-
Un Long	30	-
Chow Tau and		
Lok Ma Chow or Sun Tin	5	-
Mai Po	10	-
Chuk Yuen, Sun Wai or Fung Kat	15	-
Au Tau	20	-
Un Long	25	-

	1st Class (Cents)	2nd Class (Cents)
Lok Ma Chow or Sun Tin and		
Mai Po	5	-
Chuk Yuen, Sun Wai or Fung Kat	10	-
Au Tau	15	-
Un Long	20	-
Mai Po and		
Chuk Yuen, Sun Wai or Fung Kat	5	-
Au Tau	10	-
Un Long	15	-
Chuk Yuen, Sun Wai or Fung Kat and		
Au Tau	5	-
Un Long	10	-
Au Tau and Un Long	5	-
Fan Ling and		
On Lok or Lung Kut Tau	5	-
Kwanti	10	-
Hung Ling, Ma Mei Ha or Lai Tung	15	-
Wo Hang or Ma Chuk Kok	20	-
Sek Chung Au	25	-
Sun Chun or Sha Tau Kok	30	-
On Lok or Lung Kut Tau and		
Kwanti	5	-
Hung Ling, Ma Mei Ha or Lai Tung	10	-
Wo Hang or Ma Chuk Ling	15	-
Sek Chung Au	20	-
Sun Chun or Sha Tau Kok	25	-

	1st Class (Cents)	2nd Class (Cents)
Kwanti and		
Hung Ling, Ma Mei Ha or LeiTung	5	-
Wo Hang or Ma Chuk Ling	10	-
Sek Chung Au	15	-
Sun Chun or Sha Tau Kok	20	-
Hung Ling, Ma Mei Ha or Lai Tung and		
Wo Hang or Ma Chuk Ling	5	-
Sek Chung Au	10	-
Sun Chun or Sha Tau Kok	15	-
Wo Hang or Ma Chuk Ling and		
Sek Chung Au	5	-
Sun Chun or Sha Tau Kok	10	-
Sek Chung Au and Sun Chun or Sha Tau Kok	5	-
Fan Ling and		
Kow Lung Hang	5	-
Wai Tau	10	-
Tai Po Market	15	-
Kow Lung Hang and		
Wai Tau	5	-
Tai Po Market	10	-
Wai Tau and Tai Po Market	5	-
Kam Tin and Un Long	5	-

Appendix 2

KMB bus routes (1950s–1970s)

1950

Except for Routes 21 and 22 travelling to Clear Water Bay and Sai Kung, these routes were operated before World War II.

1965

From 1951 to 1965, routes were set up on new roads in the New Territories such as Route Twisk, Lam Kam Road, Fan Kam Road, Ping Che Road, Lau Fau Shan Road and Ting Kok Road; in urban areas, routes to Kwun Tong and Rennie's Mill (Tiu Keng Leng) were set up. KMB began providing a bus service on Lantau Island in 1960, which was terminated in 1965.

1975

Between 1966 and 1975, new routes were set up to serve new housing estates and new towns. Cross-harbour routes were also set up on the completion of the Cross-Harbour Tunnel in 1972.

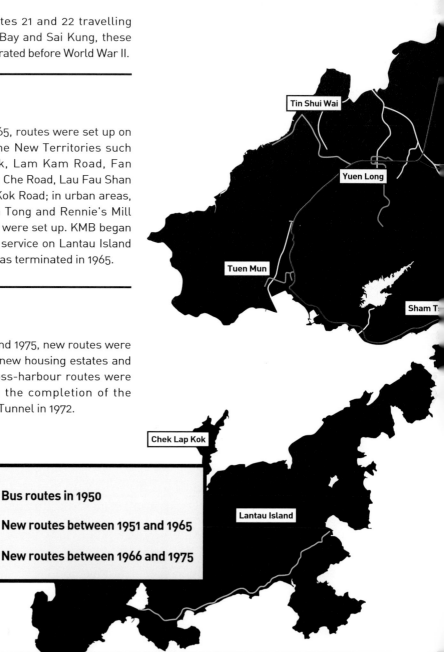

Tin Shui Wai

Yuen Long

Tuen Mun

Sham T

Chek Lap Kok

Lantau Island

———— **Bus routes in 1950**

———— **New routes between 1951 and 1965**

———— **New routes between 1966 and 1975**

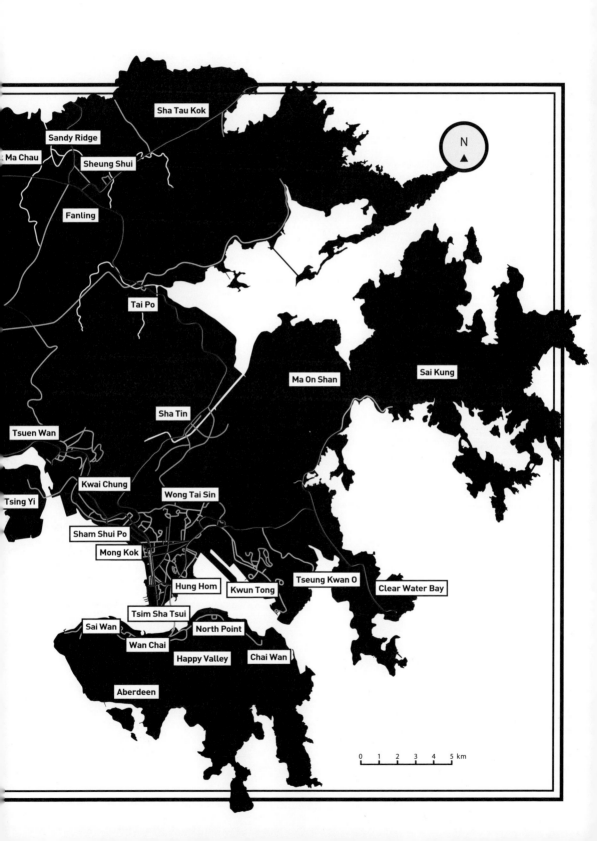

Appendix 3

KMB bus routes (2013)

2013

As of June 2013, KMB employed around 12,000 people and had a fleet of 3,800 buses operating on roughly 390 routes. The routes cover Kowloon, the New Territories and Hong Kong Island, offering approximately 2.6 million passenger trips per day.

70%

95% of the KMB fleet are double-deck buses. About 70% are super-low floor buses, the body of which can be lowered to 25cm off the ground, providing better accessibility for the disabled. KMB has the biggest super-low floor bus fleet in Hong Kong.

2,454

Every year, around 20 bus stop shelters are built and renovated. As at the end of June 2013, there were a total of 2,454 bus stop shelters.

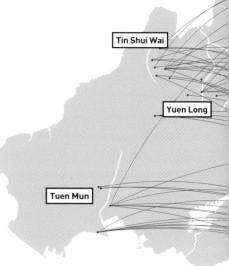

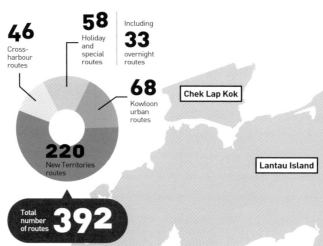

46
Cross-harbour routes

58
Holiday and special routes

Including
33
overnight routes

68
Kowloon urban routes

220
New Territories routes

Total number of routes **392**

Note: The bus route map shows KMB routes as of June 2013. Parabolic curves are used to roughly display their departure points and arrival points.

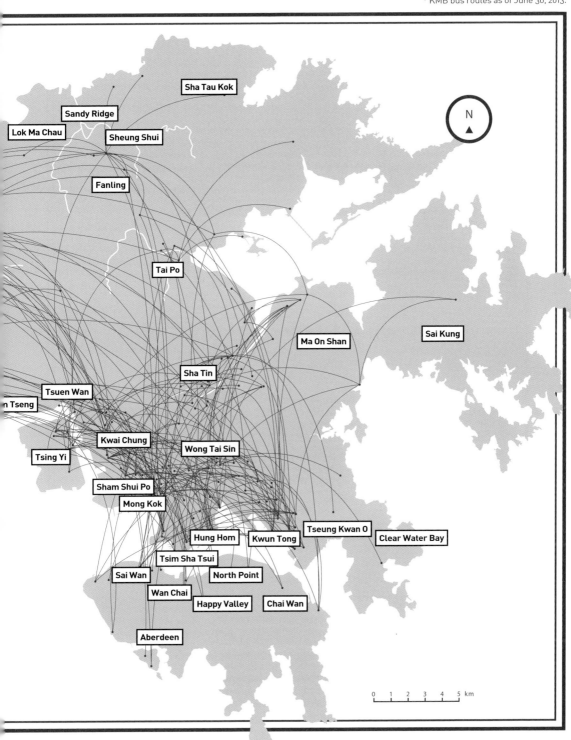

* KMB bus routes as of June 30, 2013.

Sha Tau Kok

Sandy Ridge

Lok Ma Chau

Sheung Shui

Fanling

Tai Po

Sai Kung

Ma On Shan

Sha Tin

Tsuen Wan

n Tseng

Kwai Chung

Wong Tai Sin

Tsing Yi

Sham Shui Po

Mong Kok

Tseung Kwan O

Clear Water Bay

Hung Hom

Kwun Tong

Tsim Sha Tsui

Sai Wan

North Point

Wan Chai

Happy Valley

Chai Wan

Aberdeen

N

0 1 2 3 4 5 km

Appendix 4

KMB milestones

Year	Major Developments
1921	Kowloon Motor Bus Company operated 9 Ford buses on primary routes between Tsim Sha Tsui Ferry Pier and Sham Shui Po. It also ran secondary routes between Nathan Road and Hung Hom.
1933	KMB gained the 15-year franchise to operate bus services in Kowloon and the New Territories; in April, The Kowloon Motor Bus Company (1933) Limited was founded; in June, the franchise took effect and KMB was responsible for the operation of 18 routes in Kowloon and the New Territories. The fleet consisted of 110 small single-deck buses and its depot was located on Nathan Road in Mong Kok (now the location of Pioneer Centre).
1934	The first monthly adult ticket was sold at $10 (KMB stopped issuing such tickets in September 1971) and the monthly child ticket was sold at $4 (it was changed to the half-fare ticket for students in September 1972). Ticket holders could commute a maximum of 8 times per day. Family monthly tickets were sold for $10 for 3 people, $12 for 4 people and $14 for 5 people. Family ticket holders could take unlimited rides.
1938	The number of routes dropped to 12 after reorganisation because of fuel shortages.
1941	On December 25 1941, Hong Kong surrendered to the Japanese Army. The bus fleet was employed by the Japanese military and services were paralysed.
1944	Only Route 1 still operated in Kowloon.
1945	World War II ended and the military administration of Hong Kong asked KMB to resume its bus services. At first, only 6 buses could still be used.
1946	The military government returned 8 buses to KMB which immediately operated 2 routes for the public. As many buses lacked maintenance and 30 newly-purchased buses had not been shipped, KMB converted military vehicles and lorries into buses (until the end of 1952). 7 Kowloon routes and 2 long-distance routes in the New Territories were operated by 66 buses. KMB set up its own football team nicknamed "Atomic Bus". In the 1950s, the football team was on a par with South China Athletic Association Football Team and Kitchee Football Team. The matches between KMB Football Team and South China Football Team were the talk of the town.
1947	The government announced the franchised bus services of KMB would be extended for 10 years.
1948	To meet the growing demand, KMB purchased 20 double-deck buses and 50 single-deck buses from the UK. It recorded about 56 million passenger trips; in December, to cope with the population growth of Tsuen Wan, Route 16A was set up to travel between Jordan Road Ferry Pier and Tsuen Wan. 5 routes were operated in the New Territories.
1949	In April, to cope with the population surge of Kowloon after the war, KMB operated 4 Daimler A double-deck buses on Route 1 (Tsim Sha Tsui to Kowloon City).
1953	In April, Route 23 was set up to run between Yuen Long and Tai Po Market and the number of routes in the New Territories rose to 12; bus stops were set up in rural areas in the New Territories for safety reasons and smoother operations.
1954	Doors were manned by conductors.
1957	KMB purchased 100 Seddon Mark 17 buses, which was the biggest transaction of its kind in Hong Kong. The body was assembled by KMB; the government extended the franchise of KMB until 1960. This was intended to be temporary as that would give the government more time to discuss further details with KMB.
1959	The number of Kowloon routes rose from 16 in 1952 to 28 in 1959; KMB ran 267 single-deck buses and 245 double-deck buses; training courses were provided for employees and experienced bus drivers were appointed to be instructors.

Year	Major Developments
1960	The government announced that KMB's franchise would be extended for 15 years; in October, Express Route 16B was set up to run between Jordan Road Ferry Pier and Tsuen Wan; a double-deck bus ran for the first time in the New Territories.
1961	KMB was listed on the Hong Kong Stock Exchange.
1962	The Transport Advisory Committee launched a campaign to encourage passengers to queue up.
1963	AEC Regent 5 double-deck buses were introduced. The length of the bus body was 34 feet and it was the vehicle with the highest passenger capacity (118) at the time; KMB launched campaigns to train its employees in professional etiquette; buses were gradually fitted with automatic doors.
1964	In January, a customer service hotline (862632) was set up; large-scale bus termini expanded to So Uk, Choi Hung, Wong Tai Sin, Wang Tau Hom, Hung Hom, Tsuen Wan, Yuen Long, etc. Queuing rails and waiting shelters were gradually installed; in March, the sides of double-deck buses were used for advertising.
1965	The bus depot and headquarters located at Po Lun Street, Lai Chi Kok, opened, taking over the maintenance of buses from the depot at Camp Street in Sham Shui Po; in April, Kwun Tong Depot opened. It was replaced by Kowloon Bay Depot in 1990.
1967	In May, some KMB buses were damaged or destroyed during the disturbances. There were only 6 routes in Kowloon and 5 in the New Territories providing limited services; bus services were dealt a heavy blow and employees became the target of assault. As a result, many of them quit their jobs. Many new employees were needed and training was provided for a number of posts; in early October, only 58% of bus services returned to normal; 22 female conductors were hired and their salary was the same as that of their male counterparts; the number of Kowloon routes rose from 28 in 1959 to 39 in 1967. The number of New Territories routes went up from 14 in 1961 to 26 in 1967.
1969	KMB purchased 465 new buses which were shipped and paid by instalment, including Daimler double-deckers, Seddon single-deckers and Albion single-deckers; the franchise tax rate was reduced from 20% to 15% of the total income of bus fares; in September, the operation of minibuses was legalised and posed strong competition for KMB.
1970	Dockers in the UK went on strike, causing delays to the shipment of the chassis of 50 Albion single-deckers; fares paid by section on urban routes were eliminated and the fare was universally set at 20 cents. The bus fares of 12 routes decreased and Route 40 exhibited the biggest drop, from 70 cents to 20 cents. The fares for the routes in the New Territories remained the same; the first training class for inspectors was conducted.
1971	Fares were raised for the first time in more than 20 years since the war. Monthly adult tickets, half-fares for military personnel and free rides for the Hong Kong Police, Hong Kong Auxiliary Police, Revenue Officers and postal officers were cancelled; in September, KMB received from the government a one-off grant ($5.2 million) to compensate it for losses incurred as a result of the legalisation of minibuses; in March, the number of conductors on double-deck buses was reduced from 3 to 1 with passengers required to pay the fare at the ticketing area before alighting.
1972	In August, the Cross-Harbour Tunnel opened. KMB and CMB reached an agreement and jointly-operated 3 cross-harbour routes: 101 (Kwun Tong and Kennedy Town), 102 (Lai Chi Kok and Shau Kei Wan) and 103 (Wang Tau Hom and Pokfield Road). The fare for the 3 routes was $1. By the end of the year, the routes had recorded about 12.3 million passenger trips; the last batch of the 465 buses KMB purchased in 1969 was shipped to Hong Kong; KMB also purchased 130 Daimler E double-deck buses which became the major bus model for cross-harbour routes. The cost of new buses exceeded that of old ones by 30%. Because of the dramatic increase in salaries, KMB installed fare collection boxes on buses and each vehicle was solely run by the bus driver to cut costs.

Year	Major Developments
1973	KMB employed a Chief Engineer and conducted apprenticeship programmes. It also implemented the repair and maintenance programme; it purchased the Daimler Fleetline, which was the first rear-engined bus. The bus compartment was more spacious and adopted the seating of 3x2, which raised passenger capacity; in July, Route 71 was set up to travel between Sha Tin and Jordan Road Ferry Pier.
1974	Because of raging inflation and strikes in the UK, the bus manufacturers indicated that they would only sign contracts which did not state the price of buses. The price would only be finalised and confirmed 8 months before the vehicles were shipped, which in turn delayed delivery. KMB therefore set up its own maintenance standards to meet demand; the Tyre Retreading Plant was set up which adopted the 'Bandag' process to condition the tyres.
1975	Because of serious inflation in the UK, the final price of buses was almost double the price when ordered in 1973. As the shipment of new buses was delayed, KMB had to keep operating older ones; it sent its engineers to learn about maintenance in the UK; Route 89 (Lek Yuen and Yue Man Square, Kwun Tong) and the cross-harbour Route 170 (Sha Tin and Aberdeen) were set up; 9 Kowloon routes (including 2 to and from the airport) were set up and a deluxe bus route in the New Territories, on which no passenger had to stand, was established; KMB purchased 100 Albion Viking EVK55CL buses for the deluxe bus routes. Weekend leisure routes to Tai Au Mun and Tai Mong Tsai were set up; short-distance routes to Ta Kwu Ling and Sha Tau Kok were also operated; the government announced that the franchised bus services of KMB would be extended for another 10 years. The terms and conditions mandated for the first time that KMB's internal rate of return be 16%. The government would appoint representatives for its Board of Directors. It established a development fund and the franchise was based on routes instead of districts.
1976	The Albion 55 was introduced and was KMB's last non air-conditioned single-deck bus. It mostly ran on rural routes; Kwai Chung Depot was completed and the occupation permit was obtained. It took over the machinery and repairs department that formerly belonged to To Kwa Wan Depot.
1977	Routes to Tai Tan, Nai Chung and Sai Kung were set up; the number of routes in Kowloon rose from 39 in 1967 to 68.
1978	As the cost of shipping whole buses was high, the assembly of bus parts was carried out at a depot in Tuen Mun; cross-harbour routes were popular and there were a total of 13 of them.
1979	Route 66 travelled between Tai Hing and Lai Chi Kok and it made commuting more convenient for Tuen Mun residents; Tuen Mun Depot opened to accommodate bus services in New Territories West; the first stage of MTR's Kwun Tong Line opened and the number of KMB passengers in the first 3 months dropped by 9%. The number of passengers who travelled on cross-harbour routes dropped by 20% and that of deluxe routes by 30%; to raise bus captains' awareness of safety, KMB introduced the safe driving bonus.
1980	The first 2 air-conditioned double-deck buses were introduced (Dennis Jubilant and Leyland Victory Mk 2). Since their cost was much higher than other models, they were no longer operated after a 3-year trial; the number of routes in New Territories West increased from 26 in 1967 to 57 in 1980; the number of routes in New Territories East rose from 12 in 1973 to 33 in 1980; in February, the entire Kwun Tong Line of the MTR opened and the average daily number of passengers dropped by 3.1%, compared with the previous year; the number of passengers on urban routes, cross-harbour routes and deluxe bus routes dropped by 5.5%, 19.2% and 31.3% respectively; due to the swift development of the New Territories, the number of passengers there rose by 8.4%.
1981	The 12-metre MCW Super Metrobus was introduced. In view of the growing number of passengers, the Leyland Olympian and Dennis Dragon were subsequently introduced. These double-deck buses could carry a maximum of 160 passengers, 45% more than conventional ones; good service bonuses were awarded to employees who performed well at work.
1982	The Training School was renamed the KMB Technical Training School; many new routes running between new towns and urban areas and X routes running on highways were set up; in May, the Tsuen Wan Line of the MTR opened. Initially, the number of KMB passengers dropped by 7%. The number in Tsuen Wan, urban areas, cross-harbour routes and deluxe bus routes fell by 19%, 5%, 11% and 40% respectively; with government implementation of effective schemes to alleviate traffic congestion and the development of new towns, by the end of the year the number of KMB passengers exceeded the number before the opening of the rail line; the position of conductor was eliminated and each bus was run by the bus captain alone.

Year	Major Developments
1983	KMB adopted a new logo and bus drivers were known as bus captains; the customer service hotline was computerised; the Mercedes Benz O305 was introduced mainly on express routes and it was the first time a double-deck bus made in Germany was imported into Hong Kong; in October, the KMB Overhaul Centre became operational. It was listed in the Guinness Book of Records as the largest multi-storey bus depot in the world.
1984	The training of the maintenance team intensified and 6 advanced training modules were included. Training was provided for 108 technicians and engineers.
1985	In September, KMB introduced 2 express routes in New Territories East running between Tai Po and urban areas in Kowloon; in October, air-conditioned buses were used on airport bus routes 200 and 201; the franchise was extended until August 31, 1995.
1986	KMB completed modernisation work at its bus termini, installing regulator's kiosks made of fibre glass, water tanks and rubbish bins.
1987	KMB set up many routes in Ma On Shan and Tseung Kwan O, including the 93s, 95s, 98s and 296s; in September, small air-conditioned single-deck buses were introduced.
1988	The Leyland Olympian, the world's first bus in which the air-conditioning was powered by the main engine, performed well in trials and was introduced to lead bus services into a new era; in February, the government approved the increase of minibus passenger capacity to 16. Thanks to the continuous development of new towns, there was still a great demand for bus services; in September, many routes to and from Tuen Mun and Yuen Long were terminated because of the LRT. Restrictions were also imposed so that passengers could only board or alight in designated areas. KMB lost about 130,000 passenger trips per day, a 4.4% drop; in October, the government cancelled the funding to KMB which subsidised students' fares and distributed bus passes for free. Instead, it delivered a sum to parents who resided in remote areas. As a result, KMB lost another 80,000 passenger trips per day; the franchise to operate bus services was extended until August 31, 1997; in November, Sha Tin Depot was completed and the Bus Captain Training School was established there.
1989	There was an increasing demand for bus captains. After internal consultation, KMB employed the first batch of 12 female bus captains and they operated small air-conditioned single-deckers; the first "Bus Captain of the Year" Competition was organised.
1990	The new headquarters in Lai Chi Kok opened; the number of New Territories West routes rose from 57 in 1980 to 83 in 1990; the number of New Territories East routes rose from 33 in 1980 to 86 in 1990; Kowloon Bay Depot opened, providing maintenance and parking spaces for buses on Kowloon and Tseung Kwan O routes; in May, mid-sized air-conditioned buses with a passenger capacity of 35 were introduced.
1991	Bus stop shelters made of aluminium were built and information, including route details and fares, was displayed; Shing Mun Tunnels Bus Interchange was set up and passengers who interchanged did not have to pay additional fares; seven 300s (cross-harbour routes) were set up and air-conditioned buses ran on these routes; Tate's Cairn Tunnel, the second tunnel linking Kowloon and the New Territories, opened. KMB began the operation of 4 routes which passed through the tunnel.
1992	KMB became the first public bus company in Hong Kong to install the environment-friendly Euro I bus engine, meeting the emission standards laid down by the EU (the Dennis Dragon A/C, AD53 and AD56 used the Gardner LG1200 engine); wastewater from the bus-washing process was collected and reused after treatment; in March, the government exempted KMB from fuel tax, which in turn lowered bus fares; in April, the first customer service centre was established in Sha Tin New Town Plaza for passengers to make comments or suggestions. Merchandise was also sold there.
1993	In June, the government lifted some of the restrictions imposed on the routes in the New Territories. Routes travelling between Tuen Mun and Yuen Long were allowed to let passengers board and alight at undesignated areas and section fares were introduced; the air-conditioning system was revamped and heating was provided in winter.
1994	The bus captain's name tag was displayed inside the bus compartment to bridge the gap between the bus captain and passengers.

Year	Major Developments
1995	Each row of 3x2 seating was replaced by 2x2 seating; KMB was the first public services company in Hong Kong to launch a website; it began to implement ISO9000 quality systems; trials of the Electronic Bus Stop Announcement system were carried out on buses; the "Friends of KMB" passenger club was established to encourage passengers to support charity causes with KMB.
1996	Super-low floor easy access single-deck buses (Dennis Dart SLF) were introduced; the Euro II engine was introduced to the KMB fleet (the Scania DSC11-24 engine was adopted in the Scania N113 A/C, AS3 -AS22).
1997	The world's first super-low floor double-deck bus (Dennis Trident) was introduced and it was equipped with wheelchair ramps and areas to improve accessibility for the public, particularly the disabled and the elderly; all KMB buses were also equipped with the 'Posilock' fuelling system as used on aeroplanes; the Western Harbour Tunnel opened and cross-harbour routes travelling between Northwestern New Territories and Hong Kong Island were set up; in September, the trial of the Octopus smart card payment system was carried out; the government announced the extension of KMB's franchise until July 31, 2007. It also cancelled the regulation of profits under the Scheme of Control Agreement; KMB underwent restructuring and the Kowloon Motor Bus Holdings Limited which comprised KMB, Long Win Bus Company Limited, etc. was established. The shareholders remained unchanged; seat belts were installed for seats without anything in front.
1998	In May, Tai Lam Tunnel Interchange opened; the Electronic Bus Stop Announcement system was introduced on some major routes.
1999	The ISO quality system was extended to all departments at headquarters; the Octopus Bus-Bus Interchange Discount Scheme was introduced and trials were conducted on Routes 87A and 88K; KMB gained the franchise to operate 6 bus routes in Tin Shui Wai; formal training was provided for 9,000 frontline and supporting staff to improve bus services; catalytic converters were tested and installed on older EU buses to reduce emissions of very fine particles.
2000	The number of New Territories West routes rose from 83 in 1990 to 141 in 2000; the number of New Territories East routes rose from 86 in 1990 to 130 in 2000; the first "Multi-media On-board" buses were introduced; electronic panels were installed on all buses to show the full fare and fare by section, replacing paper cards; KMB launched the point-to-point route search function on its website; bus stop shelters were renovated and materials pervious to light were used. They were also proofed against UV light, noise and heat; KMB retrofitted older buses of pre-Euro models with diesel catalytic converters to meet Euro I emission standards for exhaust particulates; electric air purifiers were used to remove contaminants from the air; catalytic converters were installed on Euro II engines and the emission of exhaust particulates was reduced by 80-90%; at the end of 2000, KMB had equipped all its buses with Octopus Card readers.
2001	All 4,000 KMB bus stops were numbered and given Chinese as well as English names; all buses used ultra-low sulphur diesel to reduce the emissions of fine particles, sulphur oxides and nitrogen oxides; in November, Sha Tin Depot received ISO 14001 certification, KMB becoming the first bus operator to receive this accreditation; KMB deployed the first bus in Hong Kong to be equipped with the Euro III engine (the Volvo D10A-285 ECO1 engine was used in the Volvo Super Olympian 3ASV141).
2002	KMB built Hong Kong's first air-conditioned passenger waiting lounge at Lam Tin Bus Terminus; it retrofitted older buses of Euro I models with diesel catalytic converters to meet the Euro II emission standards for exhaust particulates; KMB developed the pioneering Eco-Driveline on its fleet to improve engine efficiency and reduce exhaust emissions; the customer service hotline set up an enquiry system using digital maps and containing information on 100,000 landmarks. It allowed customer service operators to provide passengers with information more quickly; in May, Lai Chi Kok Depot opened; KMB recorded an average of 3.11 million passenger trips per day, the highest the bus company has recorded in its history; in August, the Tseung Kwan O Line of the MTR opened and KMB lost around 100,000 passenger trips each day.
2003	Names of en-route stops and "you are here" symbols were included in the bus stop panels displaying route information; a straight staircase, a wider bus saloon and entry way were introduced; the Electronic Terminus Management system was developed in-house by KMB to enable terminus supervisors to use Personal Data Assistants to record large volumes of operational data and deliver it to all depots and departments; in December, West Rail opened and KMB terminated and reorganised 7 routes; because of SARS and the opening of the Tseung Kwan O Line of the MTR, the daily number of passenger trips decreased by 6.5%, compared with 2002. It stood at 2.91 million.

Year	Major Developments
2004	KMB implemented the concept of green office practices by setting timers for the lighting system and temperature controllers for the air-conditioning system; in December, the Ma On Shan Line opened and KMB terminated and reorganised 4 routes. It also adjusted the frequency of 40 routes.
2005	The Kowloon Motor Bus Holdings Limited was renamed Transport International Holdings Limited; the franchise was extended until 2017 and the government introduced the Fare Adjustment Mechanism to take effect in 2006; KMB enhanced the air-conditioning system on its new buses. Thanks to intelligent temperature control and a variable compressor, the system monitored and controlled the temperature and humidity inside buses.
2006	KMB introduced 2 Euro IV environment-friendly double-deck buses to Hong Kong (the Volvo D9B-310 engine was used in the Volvo B9TL AVD1); the Electronic Bus Stop Announcement system was installed on all buses; KMB commissioned tyre recycling plants to recycle used tyres into a variety of products, including playground surfaces. It also became the first enterprise in Hong Kong to participate in the fluorescent tube recycling campaign.
2007	In December, a large-scale interchange discount scheme was introduced on a total of 21 routes, covering West Kowloon, Tsim Sha Tsui, Tsuen Wan, Sham Tseng, Kwai Ching, Sha Tin, Tai Po, Yuen Long, Hung Shui Kiu, Tuen Mun and New Territories North. KMB had 68 combinations of 258 routes in the discount scheme; KMB adopted the use of Euro V Diesel with a sulphur content of 0.001%; the Driving Simulator Studio was introduced to simulate real-world driving environments to train bus captains and improve their decision-making abilities and performance; with the merging of the MTR and KCR, some stations were renamed; KMB launched the first boundary service, Route B1, running between Yuen Long West Rail Station and Lok Ma Chau Spur Line Bus Terminus; because of the railways, the daily number of passenger trips dropped to 2.76 million.
2008	The daily number of passenger trips further dropped to 2.7 million because of the financial crisis. As the unemployment rate rose and the economy weakened, the demand for public transport plunged.
2009	KMB introduced the first double-deck bus with a Euro V engine (the ADL Enviro 500 and ATEU1 originally used the Cummins ISLe340b Euro IV engine then switched to the Cummins ISL8.9e5340b Euro V engine); large-scale customer service training was launched, encouraging over 10,000 employees to strive for better services; luminous crystal bus-stop poles were introduced to help passengers check route information more conveniently; KMB launched the database of "Driving Tips in Special Attention Areas"; the Kowloon Southern Link of the MTR opened and the daily number of KMB passenger trips fell to 2.64 million.
2010	In July, KMB carried out trials on Hong Kong's first zero-emission electric bus powered by supercapacitor technology, gBus; it introduced the street view function on the company website, providing a 360-degree virtual tour of the streets; in September, the Safety and Service Quality Department was set up to identify key challenges for safe bus operations and implement initiatives to strengthen safety risk management.
2011	Mobile apps for iPhone and Android were launched; 4 priority seats were designated on each bus to encourage passengers to give their seats to those in need.
2012	In April, KMB carried out the trial of gBus^2 powered by supercapacitor technology; in May, the last batch of non air-conditioned buses retired (Dennis Dragon and Volvo Olympian); in October, KMB received OHSAS18001 certification, becoming the first road transport company to receive the accreditation; in December, KMB spent $100 million on 370 ADL Enviro 500 MMC double-deckers which could reduce the consumption of diesel and carbon emissions by 10%. The air-conditioning was also improved; room was reserved on the chassis for the future development of the Euro VI and hybrid diesel-electric engines; the Tuen Mun Road Bus-Bus Interchange opened and the pioneering Estimated Time of Arrival System was introduced.
2013	In January, the Chief Executive announced that the reorganisation of bus routes was his focus as far as public transport policies were concerned. In the same month, KMB carried out Hong Kong's first consultations in North District regarding area-based reorganisation of bus routes and will do the same in other districts in the near future; in April, to celebrate its 80th anniversary, KMB organised a grand ceremony and carnival which was attended by 26,000 guests.

Appendix 5

KMB's Organisational chart

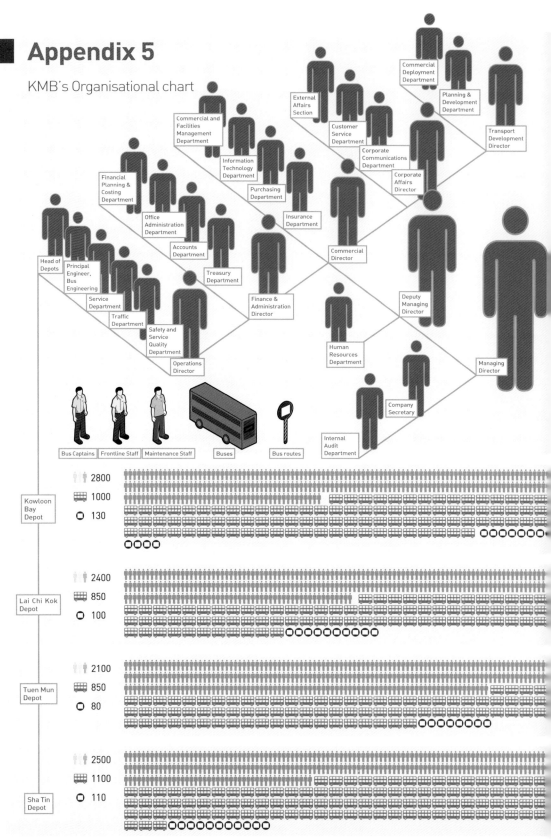

Kowloon Bay Depot	2800	1000	130
Lai Chi Kok Depot	2400	850	100
Tuen Mun Depot	2100	850	80
Sha Tin Depot	2500	1100	110

Note 1: Estimated numbers are shown in the chart.   Note 2: Each symbol represents 10 units.

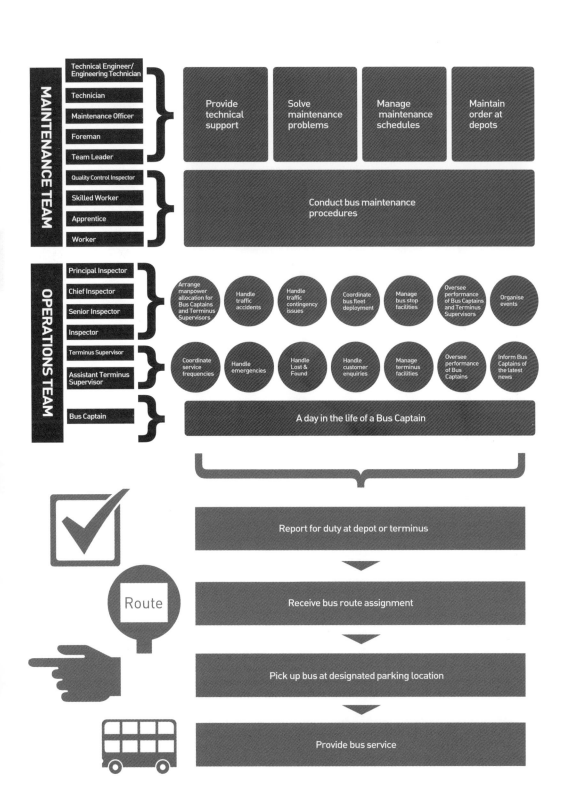

MAINTENANCE TEAM

- Technical Engineer/ Engineering Technician
- Technician
- Maintenance Officer
- Foreman
- Team Leader

Provide technical support

Solve maintenance problems

Manage maintenance schedules

Maintain order at depots

- Quality Control Inspector
- Skilled Worker
- Apprentice
- Worker

Conduct bus maintenance procedures

OPERATIONS TEAM

- Principal Inspector
- Chief Inspector
- Senior Inspector
- Inspector

Arrange manpower allocation for Bus Captains and Terminus Supervisors

Handle traffic accidents

Handle traffic contingency issues

Coordinate bus fleet deployment

Manage bus stop facilities

Oversee performance of Bus Captains and Terminus Supervisors

Organise events

- Terminus Supervisor
- Assistant Terminus Supervisor

Coordinate service frequencies

Handle emergencies

Handle Lost & Found

Handle customer enquiries

Manage terminus facilities

Oversee performance of Bus Captains

Inform Bus Captains of the latest news

- Bus Captain

A day in the life of a Bus Captain

Report for duty at depot or terminus

Route

Receive bus route assignment

Pick up bus at designated parking location

Provide bus service

Appendix 6

The floor plan of a KMB depot

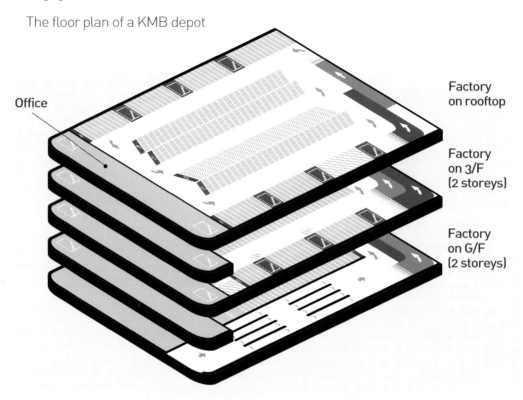

Office

Factory
on rooftop

Factory
on 3/F
(2 storeys)

Factory
on G/F
(2 storeys)

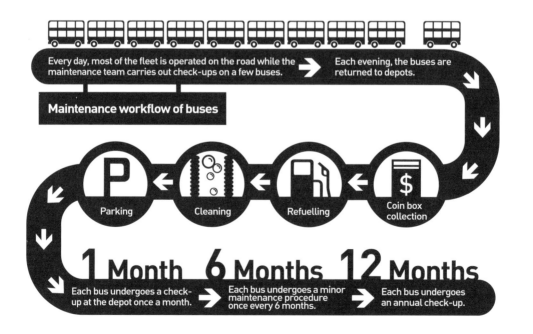

Every day, most of the fleet is operated on the road while the maintenance team carries out check-ups on a few buses.

Each evening, the buses are returned to depots.

Maintenance workflow of buses

Parking

Cleaning

Refuelling

Coin box collection

1 Month   **6** Months   **12** Months

Each bus undergoes a check-up at the depot once a month.

Each bus undergoes a minor maintenance procedure once every 6 months.

Each bus undergoes an annual check-up.

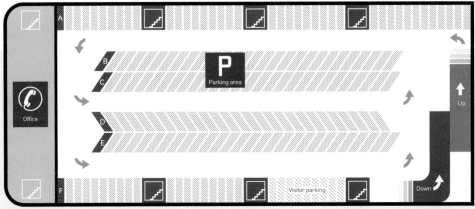

Parking area of rooftop factory

No. of parking spaces: 211

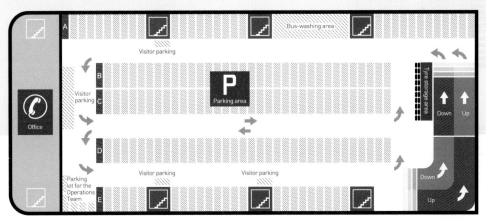

Parking area of 3/F factory

No. of parking spaces: 185

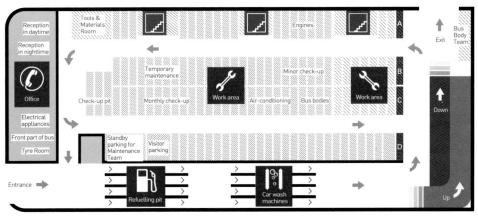

Parking area of G/F factory

No. of working pits: 63   No. of working spaces: 37

Appendix 7

Bus models

Daimler

1. Daimler A
   1949-1983

2. Daimler B
   1959-1984

3. Daimler C
   1962-1987

4. Daimler D
   1967-1988

5. Daimler E
   1969-1991

6. Daimler F
   1969-1988

7. Daimler Fleetline CRG6
   1974-1995

8. Daimler Fleetline FE33AGR
   1976-1995

9. Daimler Fleetline CRL6
   1981-1990

Leyland

1. Lion PLSCI
1926-1930

2. Albion VT17L
1961-1987

3. Albion VT23L
1963-1984

4. Albion CH13AXL
1965-1987

5. Albion EVK41XL
1970-1990

6. Albion EVK55CL & ECK41L
1976-1992

7. Albion Coach
1975-1988

8. Titan PD3/5
1973-1981

9. Victory II A/C
1981-1983

10. Leyland Olympian B45
1981-1999

11. Atlantean
1973-1979

12. Guy Victory II
1976-1998

13. Leyland Olympian 9.5M
1983-2002

14. Leyland Olympian 11M
1986-2011

15. Leyland Olympian A/C 11M
1990-2011

16. Leyland Olympian 12M
1982-2003

M. C. W

1. Metrorider
   1988-1993

2. M. C. W. 9.7M
   1983-2003

3. M. C. W. 11M
   1986-2007

4. M. C. W. A/C 11M
   1987-1989

5. M. C. W. 12M
   1981-1996

Volvo

1. Volvo B10MD
   1984-1988

2. Volvo Olympian 11M
   1995-2012

3. Volvo Olympian A/C 11M
   1994-

4. Volvo Olympian A/C 12M
   1994-

5. Volvo Super Olympian A/C 10.6M
   2001-

6. Volvo Super Olympian A/C 12M
   1999-

7. Volvo B9TL 12M
   2004-

8. Volvo B7RLE MCV Euro V 12M
   2010-

Dennis

1. Pax
1952-1969

2. Dart 9M (Cartyle)
1992-2008

3. Dart 10M (Duple Metsec)
1993-2011

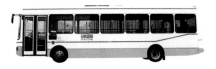

4. Dart 10M (Northern Countries)
1995-

5. Dart 10M SLF (Plaxton Pointer)
1996-

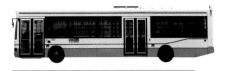

6. Dart (Twin-door) 10.7M
2003-

7. Falcon
1985-2001

8. Jubilant 9.7M
1977-2000

9. Jubilant A/C 9.7M
   1980-1983

10. Dominator 9.5M
    1983-2001

11. Dragon A/C 10M
    1993-

12. Dragon A/C 11M
    1990-

13. Dragon A/C 12M
    1997-

14. Lance 11.7M
    1993-2010

15. Trident 12M
    1997-

16. Dragon 11M
    1987-2012

17. Dragon 12M
   1982-2003

18. Trident 10.6M
   1999-

19. Trident Enviro 500 12M
   2003-

20. ADL Enviro 400 Euro V 10.5M
   2010-

21. Dart E200 Euro V 10.4M
   2011-

22. Trident E500 Turbo Euro V 12M
   2013-

Others

1. Commer Superpoise
   1934-1965

2. Dodge G5
   1946-1955

3.Thornysroft CD4LW
   1934-1950

4. Tilling Stevens
   1947-1969

5. Ford Thames Trader
   1961-1969

6. Bedfort O. B.
   1946-1959

7. Bedford S. B. O.
   1956-1970

8. Bedford Y. R. Q.
   1975-1980

9. Seddon Mk17
1957-1971

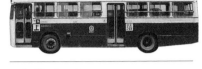

10. Seddon Pennine
1970-1980

11. A. E. C Regent V
1963-1987

12. Toyota Coaster
1987-1997

13. Mitsubishi MK117
1990-2011

14. Mitsubishi MK217
1995-2012

15. Mitsubishi MK218
1996-2002

16. Mitsubishi MP618
1993-1994

17. Hino
    1990-1993

18. Mercedes-Benz O 305
    1983-2002

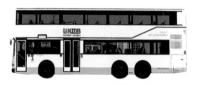

19. Scania A/C N113
    1993-

20. Scania K310UD EURO IV
    2007-

21. Neoplan Centroliner N4026
    1998-

22. Neoplan Centroliner N4426
    2001-

23. MAN 12M
    2000-

24. Neo-Man 12M
    2003-

25. Scania K230 UB 10.6M
   2009-

26. Scania K230 UB 12M
   2009-

Acknowledgements

(In no particular order)

Mr Richard Y.S. Tang

Dr Joseph Ting Sun-pao

Mr Cheng Po Hung

Mr Charles Lui Chung Yuen

Dr John Chan Cho Chak

Mr Wong Lam

Mr Sin Sing

Mr Camillus Woo Kin Keung

Mr Lai Ping Kwong

Mr Leung Yat Fan

Mr Chiu Man Kuen

Ms Siu Kar Lie

Ms Kong Wai Mui

Mr Cheng Yuk Man

Ms Leung Mei Fan

Mr Lam Pak Kay

Mr Louis Ho Kwok Bui

Ms Kirsty Norman

Mr Mike Davis

Mr Philippe Van Hoof

Mr Andrew Suddaby